PRAISE FOR
*THE WESTERN GUIDE TO FENG SHUI—ROOM BY ROOM*

*"Terah's new book belongs on that small shelf reserved for Feng Shui classics. It's an absolute must for anyone who wants to see virtually every area of their life improve as they enhance each room of their home. I highly recommend it!"*

— Barbara Harwood, founder of Enviro Custom Homes;
author of *The Healing House: How Living in the Right
House Can Heal You Spiritually, Emotionally, and Physically*

*"Terah Kathryn Collins has completely transformed the way I think about, and live in, my home. Let this book inspire you to create a personal paradise in which to grow and thrive."*

— Christiane Northrup, M.D.,
author of *Women's Bodies, Women's Wisdom*

*"Terah Kathryn Collins has outdone herself—again. I expected to use this book for reference and instead read it like a novel, not wanting to put it down until I'd read every inviting word."*

— Victoria Moran,
author of *Shelter for the Spirit* and *Creating a Charmed Life*

# THE WESTERN GUIDE TO
# FENG SHUI
## *Room by Room*

# THE WESTERN GUIDE TO
# FENG SHUI
## *Room by Room*

### *Terah Kathryn Collins*

**HAY HOUSE, INC.**
Carlsbad, California
London • Sydney • Johannesburg
Vancouver • Hong Kong • New Delhi

**Published and distributed in the United States by:** Hay House, Inc.: www.hayhouse.com •
**Published and distributed in Australia by:** Hay House Australia Pty. Ltd.:
www.hayhouse.com.au • **Published and distributed in the United Kingdom by:** Hay House
UK, Ltd.: www.hayhouse.co.uk • **Published and distributed in the Republic of South
Africa by:** Hay House SA (Pty), Ltd.: orders@psdprom.co.za • **Distributed in Canada by:**
Raincoast: www.raincoast.com • **Published in India by:** Hay House Publishers India:
www.hayhouseindia.co.in

*Editorial:* Jill Kramer          *Design:* Jenny Richards

The author of this book does not dispense medical advice or prescribe the use of any technique as a form of treatment for physical or medical problems without the advice of a physician, either directly or indirectly. The intent of the author is only to offer information of a general nature to help you in your quest for emotional and spiritual well-being. In the event you use any of the information in this book for yourself, which is your constitutional right, the author and the publisher assume no responsibility for your actions.

**Library of Congress Cataloging-in-Publication Data**

Collins, Terah Kathryn.
      The western guide to feng shui : room by room / Terah Kathryn
Collins
          p.     cm.
      Includes bibliographical references.
      ISBN 1-56170-568-3 (alk. paper)
      1. Feng-shui.  2. Interior decoration.  I.  Title.
BF1779.F4C66   1999
133.3'337–dc21                     99-11957
                                           CIP

ISBN 13: 978-1-56170-568-9
ISBN 10: 1-56170-568-3

10  09  08  07    24  23  22  21
1st printing, August 1999
21st printing, March 2007

Printed in the United States of America

## To those of you who:

*Do all the good you can*
*By all the means you can*
*In all the ways you can*
*In all the places you can*
*At all the times you can*
*For all the people you can*
*As long as ever you can*

— John Wesley's Rule

# Contents

- Closets and Bureaus—Pockets of Plenty
- The Television in the Bedroom—Who's Watching Whom?
- Directional Sleeping
- Master Bedrooms
- Children's Bedrooms
- Single People's Bedrooms
- Guest Rooms
- Quick Reference Guidelines for Bedrooms

- Follow Your Bliss
- Claiming Your Space
- Quick Reference Guidelines for the Sanctuary

- Close the Drains or Close the Doors
- Meaningful Motifs
- Bathroom Bagua
- Quick Reference Guidelines for Bathrooms

- Quick Reference Guidelines for the Laundry Room and Garage

- Enlighten Your Belongings
- Quick Reference Guidelines for Storage Areas

- Quick Reference Guidelines for Hallways and Stairways

# Preface

This book is a dream come true for me; I've always loved the way that a picture can say a thousand words. While my first book, *The Western Guide to Feng Shui,* contains charts and simple line drawings; and my second, *Home Design with Feng Shui A–Z* (a condensed version of this book), is colorfully illustrated, the opportunity to capture Feng Shui with a camera was a goal I'd long envisioned. Fortunately, I had no idea what a time-consuming adventure it would be. If I had known, I might have declined the experience of a lifetime. For all the work, time, and effort it took, it was more than worth it—it brought a dream to life.

It was also great fun. I included people in some of the shots to underscore the fact that these homes are real. People actually do live here! Their enthusiasm and willingness to "get into it" made many of our photo shoots more like a party than work. In the dining room photograph, Figure 7A on page 135, for instance, our models were having such a good time that we couldn't get their attention for the shot. What you see is their spontaneous enjoyment of the moment. I couldn't have directed them better if I'd tried.

Although black-and-white photographs are used to illustrate the main part of the text, it was vital to duplicate some of them in color with the same captions in the middle of the book. After all, we live in a world of color, and color is one of the primary tools used in Feng Shui to enhance a home. In fact, when you compare the black-and-white with the color photographs, it really "brings it home" how much color adds to our lives.

All of the photos were taken in the San Diego area and document real conditions found in typical Western homes. Solutions to Feng Shui challenges were chosen by the client based on budget and personal taste, and with few exceptions, they were in place long before we photographed them. As you look at the photos, decide what you might have done in a similar situation. The personal nature of the solution is always an important part of its power. Feng Shui guidelines for achieving harmony are flexible enough to support your personal needs, conditions, and preferences. Even the Feng Shui basics, such as the Bagua Map, Five Elements, and Ch'i Enhancements, are subject to personal interpretation. Always, it's the results that count. Trust yourself, and enjoy the ever-unfolding process of creating a heavenly life, thought by thought, moment by moment, room by room.

# $\mathscr{A}cknowledgments$

There is a band of angels in my life who made writing this book possible. They are the life-savers, the miracle workers, the bright lights who have blessed me with their support and encouragement in writing about my passion—Feng Shui. I am blessed and grateful to know you.

To Linda Carter, Jackie and Richard Earnest, Elaine and Terry Hailwood, Louise Hay, Jeff Kahn, Mary Lou LoPreste, Dan McFarland and Barbara Takashima, Barbara Masters and Alan Richards, Bob Petrello, Bidyut and Uday Sengupta, and Ron Tillinghast for opening your homes to our Feng Shui camera. The very foundation of this book was built on your complete generosity and enthusiasm. Thank you.

To Cheryl Rice, true soul buddy and interior designer extraordinaire, whose talents in creating Feng Shui–savvy environments are seen in several of the homes in this book.

To the artists whose original works appear throughout the book. Thank you Monte deGraw in Solana Beach, CA; Jan Gorden with Ballard's in Atlanta, GA; Karen Haughey of Fremont, CA; Lynn Hays in Del Mar, CA; Louise Hoffman in Las Vegas, NV; Richard Haeger of Encinitas, CA; Brett Hesser of San Diego, CA; Jeff Kahn in Encinitas, CA; Jacki Powell in La Mesa, CA; Cheryl Rice Interiors in La Jolla, CA; and the artists represented by Trios Gallery in Solana Beach, CA: Dan Diaz, James Hubbell, Alex Long, Sally Pearce, Geri Scalone, Karin Swildens, and Charles Thomas. Each of you inspires the creative spirit within us all.

Thank you Becky Iott, Linda Kay, Jennifer Moy, Jane Ozuna, and Duana Wanket for contributing your masterful energies to the Western School of Feng Shui. It is because of you that the school grows, prospers, and can offer Feng Shui education to our global community.

And to my students and clients who keep my Feng Shui eyes wide open and enjoying every minute of it, thank you for fueling my passion by sharing it with me.

Thanks also to Shelley Anderson; David and Amita Bardwick; Adam Barton; Alice, Carol, and Klint Beatson; Martina Chapkis; Cathy Coleman; Kurt Congdon; Ray Egan; Kovida and Tony Fisher; Diane Grover; Ebba Hansen; Brooke, Robert, and Logan Harvey; the entire Hay House Publishing gang; Alice Hetzel; Apara Kohls; Shivam Kohls; Randal McEndree; Evana Maggiore; Alan Miller; Mimi Miller; Marti, Ron, and Paul Luc Montbleau; Bill Ozuna; Karen and Gary Pooler; Candy Rojas; Ellen Schneider; Dale, Blanca, and Julia Schusterman; Margot Shia; Bridget Skinner; Rosemary and Charley Stokes; Evelyn "ET" Thomas; Greg Verhey; and Heather Williams. Your love and friendship throughout the many-splendored writing process has been a constant source of support and inspiration.

My gratitude and admiration also to Christopher Alexander, Don Aslett, Louis Audet, Thomas Bender, Sarah Ban Breathnach, Carol Bridges, Deepak Chopra, Isle Crawford, Wayne Dyer, Dennis Fairchild, Louise Hay, Karen Kingston, Anthony Lawlor, Jami Lin, Denise Linn, Victoria Moran, James Allyn Moser, Christiane Northrup, Arnold Patent, James and Salle Redfield, Sarah Rossbach, Mona Lisa Schulz, William Spear, Dr. Richard Tan, Carol Venolia, Rich Welt, and Professor Lin Yun for your talent and inspiration as writers, teachers, and contributors to environmental harmony.

And always, to my husband, Brian Collins. Thank you for your brilliant content editing on this book, as well as your tender loving care in making sure I ate, slept, and had regular doses of fun while working on it. You are my best friend, my heart's desire, and essentially, the loving force behind my every word.

# *Introduction*

# JOINING THE
# SEEN AND THE
# UNSEEN FORCES
# OF NATURE

*"We are what we think. All that we are arises with our thoughts. With our thoughts, we make the world."*
— Buddha

When asked to define *Feng Shui,* I often begin by saying that it is "the study of how to arrange your environment to enhance the quality of your life." But the most accurate definition of Feng Shui isn't in a line. It's in a circle that is constantly turning, each rotation building upon the one before it to achieve perfect harmony. So the definition of Feng Shui might look like the circle of words on the next page:

**FIGURE IA**

Feng Shui is the study of how to arrange your outer world to enhance your inner world to enhance your outer world to enhance your inner world to enhance your outer world to enhance your inner world to enhance your outer world to enhance your inner world to enhance your outer world to enhance your inner world to enhance your outer world to enhance your inner world to enhance your outer world...

Feng Shui, translated as "Wind and Water," observes the relationship between the seen and unseen forces of nature. Like wind and water, you and your environment are two forces of nature. Your desires, goals, talents, attitudes, and feelings—like the unseen force of wind; and the home environment you live in—like the seen force of water; are constantly interacting and influencing each other. And as with wind and water, when you and your home blend harmoniously, the effect is friendly, comfortable, and positive. Life is replete with fair weather conditions such as abundant resources, good relations, and a steady stream of opportunities. In such harmonious circumstances, your health, prosperity, and happiness thrive.

On the other hand, when you and your home clash in some way, extreme conditions prevail. Your life's weather pattern may include a "stagnant" job, a "stormy" marriage, a "drought" of resources, or a "flood" of health problems. The primary goal of Feng Shui is to bring you and your home into harmony so that you are not just *surviving* one storm after another, but are *thriving* in a paradise of your own design.

Over the past decade, joining forces with my home has transformed my life. When the wind of my clear intention sweeps across the water of my environment, change happens. Feng Shui can show you how to join forces with your home so that all heaven can break loose in your life. To do so means creating an intimate union between you and your home. It's a marriage waiting to happen.

### Form and Compass—the Two Basic Schools of Feng Shui

The philosophical foundation of Feng Shui is as relevant today in our Western culture as it was thousands of years ago in China. The two primary schools of Feng Shui, the Form School and the Compass School, while cut from the same philosophical mold, appear quite different. Form School Feng Shui focuses on the arrangement of "forms" or objects in and around a household to achieve optimal Ch'i—vital energy—flow. This school of Feng Shui is more of a fine art than a strict science and is very flexible in meeting needs and honoring personal tastes of clients while improving Ch'i flow.

Compass School Feng Shui relies on the use of a *luo pan*, or Chinese compass, and the birth information of homeowners to assess environments. Based on numerical findings, the Compass school is especially useful when you are building your own home and can choose where to place rooms, doors, and windows. Subgroups spawned by both Form and Compass Schools have added their own interpretations and practices, so you'll find that Feng Shui practitioners vary widely in the way they practice.

Over the years, I've observed that Form School techniques produce excellent results and are generally easier to integrate into the Western lifestyle. Out of my observations and experiences, I've developed Essential Feng Shui™, which takes a very practical and personalized approach to bringing the benefits of Feng Shui into our Western environments.

### As Within, So Without—a New Way of Seeing

I've worked with people from all walks of life, living in all kinds of homes—from huge mansions to suburban tract houses and small apartments. With few exceptions, they call me because they're unhappy—there is something about their lives that isn't working. They may be getting divorced, have chronic health problems, or hate their jobs. They may be tormented by the past, confused by the present, or scared of the future. Whatever the challenge, I introduce them to a new way of seeing and addressing their woes. Until their Feng Shui appointments, most of my clients thought their emotional and spiritual lives were completely separate from their home environments. The Feng Shui premise that happiness and environment are two forces of nature "who" are intimately connected is a brand new idea for them. The realization that their homes can literally strengthen or weaken their health, wealth, and happiness brings with it a significant shift in perception.

When these individuals open their Feng Shui eyes, they can no longer view their homes as just "things" or their belongings as just inanimate "stuff." Their homes, and all the possessions within them, suddenly come alive and are intimately connected to their quality of life. They see that their difficulties are not separate from, but actually held *in place by,* their homes. Thus, the vital connection between the people and the "beings" they call home begins. As they embrace their connection with their homes, feelings of isolation and disconnection transform into personal power and creativity. The "wind" of their intentions becomes purposeful as it's directed across the "water" of their homes. This brings the seen and the unseen forces into harmony, and as a result, life changes for the better.

As a holistic art and science, Feng Shui is meant to balance and harmonize your inner and outer domains. In our culture, as Feng Shui has become more popular, so has the tendency to make it strictly an outer "quick fix" practice. I see all kinds of Feng Shui embellishments popping up in people's homes that are supposed to create instant cash, jobs, or love. People stand back, arms crossed over their chests, feet tapping, impatiently waiting for Santa Feng Shui to magically appear. They don't realize that *they* breathe "the magic" into the changes they want in life. Their embellishments remain like a still pool, until touched by the vital breath of intention and focus. Only then, when their purpose and clarity join forces with their enhancements, will positive and lasting changes occur.

### From Popcorn to Prosperity

One of my favorite stories involves a bowl of popcorn I found on the back of my client Pam's toilet. She had read an article on Feng Shui that said that wealth would be multiplied by putting popcorn in the bathroom. Weird as it was, she decided to try it. Her family needed a financial boost, and something always seemed to prevent her from moving forward and returning to work. Maybe the popcorn would do the trick. After several weeks with no perceivable results, she decided to have a Feng Shui consultation to get to the bottom of all this. When I arrived, we went straight to the bathroom, where she asked me to explain exactly how damp, stale popcorn was going to multiply her wealth.

I explained to Pam that her Feng Shui "cure" originated from the study of the Five Elements. The popcorn, representing the Wood element, was meant to balance the overabundance of the Water element in a bathroom, which in turn balanced the flow of money and resources in life. If she really wanted to increase her wealth, however, it was going to take more than putting a bowl of popcorn on the toilet. To receive full benefit, Pam needed to join forces with her entire home and add her clear intention and focus to the formula. As she did so, she could choose enhancements and arrange the house to invite wealth in all its forms to flow into her life. In the meantime, there were many ways to bring the Wood element into the bathroom, including plants; flowers; floral and striped designs on towels, curtains, and wallpaper; and the colors of blue and green. It didn't have to be popcorn, which she was quite relieved to hear.

As is often the case, Pam's home needed a lot more outer work than one enhancement in the bathroom. The lack of prosperity she was experiencing showed up in every room. We made a long list of environmental and corresponding internal changes she could make to improve the Feng Shui of her home and her life. Over the next few weeks, she looked through new eyes at the rooms in her home and began to change them to accurately reflect her stated intention to "let go of poverty consciousness, move forward, and embrace prosperity consciousness."

Pam started at her front entrance, where she placed a fountain to symbolize an abundant flow of resources and opportunities streaming into the house. She removed a table that partially blocked the front door, and rearranged the living room, affirming her willingness to open up and be prosperous. A journal by her bedside reminded her to think about who and what she was grateful for, and to add to her "bank account" of positive thoughts.

She also cleared out useless junk "parked" in the garage, and organized bikes and tools to make plenty of room for the cars. For the first time in years, the vehicles had a home *inside* the garage, and not just *on* the driveway, and Pam felt as though she had some real control over her life. Cleaning out the garage symbolized her letting go of the worthless to make room for the priceless; priorities were getting straight. She unpacked the sparkling crystal candleholders that had always been "too good" to use and placed them on the living room mantel to symbolize with crystal clarity her growing sense of prosperity.

Room by room, Pam let go of possessions that made her feel poor, including old, broken, and extra stuff she'd kept around "just in case." She displayed favorite belongings that reminded her that wealth comes in myriad forms. The house was becoming a lighter, more joyful place to be. All except one room—her home office. She'd saved the most challenging for last. To complete her Feng Shui work, Pam knew that she needed to face it and reclaim the part of her life it represented.

Known as the "junk room," homeless possessions camped in every corner and surface of the room. Suddenly it was no mystery why she never got any work done in there. Box after box, Pam cleared out what didn't belong—hamster cages, Halloween costumes, hundreds of catalogs, suitcases, the kids' old homework and outgrown clothes—and she organized the rest. With room to maneuver, she placed her desk so that she could see the door from the desk chair. When she surveyed the room from her new vantage point, Pam felt completely exhilarated and empowered. The room was singing, and for the first time that she could remember, she felt prosperous to her core. This was the reflection of herself she wanted to see; this was how she wanted to feel. All the other changes in the house had made a difference, but this one was transformational. Pam crossed in consciousness from rags to riches.

From that moment on, she was drawn to her office. And unlike before, work poured in, bringing Pam a steady flow of lucrative opportunities in her field of medical sales. Meanwhile, every time her husband parked in the garage, he complimented her on how wonderful she was. Her children seemed to calm down and get along with each other better than ever before. And, eventually, Pam got around to putting floral towels and several plants in the bathroom.

The popcorn on the toilet marked the beginning of her Feng Shui adventure. From that point forward, Pam joined forces with her home, and step by step, she brought harmony to her seen and unseen worlds. Now her favorite saying is "Another day in paradise."

### Feng Shui Acts of Courage

It is a real act of courage to open your Feng Shui eyes and take a detailed look at what your home is saying about you. It usually leads to extraordinary insights, immediate calls to action, and deeply empowering inner and outer changes. Your discoveries can also be exhausting and overwhelming. As you correlate the arrangement of your home with your goals and desires, you recognize what's strengthening and enhancing— or weakening and detracting from—your well-being.

In the story above, my client saw reflections of her "poverty consciousness" right in the middle of several rooms in the house. She realized that she couldn't just open her Feng Shui eyes once, gaze briefly into the looking glass that was her home, then close her eyes again and live happily ever after. To heal and strengthen herself, she had to step fully into the looking glass and participate. To thrive, she needed to change the areas and belongings in her home "who" held in place the confusion, tension, and poverty of her inner life. Each room presented her with an opportunity to see herself. When she didn't like what she saw, she changed it for the better, making her home a place that constantly encouraged and enhanced her prosperity, joy, and power. This was an act of courage.

# Chapter One

# FENG SHUI PRINCIPLES AND GUIDELINES TO LIVE BY

*"We are caught in an inescapable network of mutuality, tied in a single garment of destiny. Whatever affects one directly, affects all indirectly."*
— Martin Luther King, Jr.

Three basic principles make up the foundation of Feng Shui and provide us with guidelines for living. When we integrate these guidelines into our lives, we see and interact with the world in a new and very powerful way.

### Feng Shui Principle I—Everything Is Alive with Ch'i

The first principle in the Feng Shui philosophy is that every person, place, and thing is alive with the vital energy we call Ch'i. This concept is all-inclusive, changing our physical existence from a world "that" is largely inanimate to a world "who" is completely alive.

When we see our world as made up of animate "beings," we make decisions differently than when we see things as inanimate. Indiscriminate destruction of our natural world, as well as amassing large quantities of possessions we don't love or need, can only happen when we believe it's just "dirt" or "stuff." When we feel the aliveness of all things around us, including the earth beneath our feet and the belongings that surround us, we are compelled to be *care-full*. We tend to slow down, treating ourselves, each other, nature, and our belongings with dignity, knowing that every "thing" is imbued with vital energy.

**Expanding Your Sense of Aliveness:** When I first studied Feng Shui, I knew that my friends and houseplants were alive, but I didn't realize that everything else, including my artwork, furniture, linens, clothes, shoes, computer, car, and jewelry were also alive. I went from having a bunch of inanimate stuff to being surrounded by a large group of living things. Entwined with the dancing molecules in my belongings were my thoughts, feelings, memories, and associations with each and every one of them. I couldn't move in my house without receiving impressions from the possessions that surrounded me—impressions that for a moment in time enhanced or detracted from my experience of life.

For instance, in my kitchen is a wooden table that was my grandmother's. Along with the molecular makeup of the wood itself, the table is alive with warm memories of my grandmother's kitchen and her loving presence throughout my childhood. I can still see my sister sitting up very straight at the table on Saturday mornings and ordering mashed potatoes and ice cream for breakfast, which my grandmother cheerfully gave her every time. We had countless tea parties around the table, complete with our choice of teacup from Grannie's bone china collection.

The table continues to collect memories of everyday life in my own kitchen. When I sit at the table, dozens of recollections and feelings spring to mind: lazy Sunday mornings with the paper spread out across the top, making collages with friends, and quiet suppers in the warm glow of candlelight. These memories and feelings strengthen me, and remind me to relax and enjoy the stream of precious moments in my life.

Everything that lives with you holds certain memories, associations, and feelings in place. That's why it's so vital in Feng Shui to assess what your material possessions are alive with. What are they "saying" to you? The quality of your inner life is constantly influenced by what you're keeping alive in your surroundings. Like my table, the feelings and memories may be of good times and delicious moments. Or, they may carry a mixed message.

I have a book of poetry that was a gift from a friend long ago. I cherish the book, love the poetry, and have fond memories of my friend. However, he and several other friends died in an auto accident a few years ago. So when I look at the book, I feel both love and loss. It was important for me to weigh whether the feelings and memories kept alive by the book promote my sense of well-being now, or drag me down. In this case, the book keeps the memory of my friend alive, and I like that. Therefore, I choose to keep the book, knowing that my energy is strengthened every time I see it.

There are other times when this is not the case. For instance, when my friend Susan began to wade through a complicated divorce, her living room sofa became a war zone of associations. Every time she sat on it, a flood of discordant memories besieged her. She was the happy newlywed and the shell-shocked divorcée all at the same time. The sofa was alive with her feelings about her marriage, and the marriage was history—everywhere but in her mind, emotions, and living room. Susan's inner work consisted of letting go of the past and healing her bruised self-image. Her outer work, in this case, was to buy a new couch!

She chose a new piece "who" was alive with the Ch'i of new beginnings. As soon as the couch was delivered, Susan felt far more in control of her life. She was amazed at how it affirmed a new chapter in her life. It was much easier for her to relax, enjoy the moment, and release the past. This spurred her on to question other possessions that kept memories and feelings alive that she didn't want around anymore. She put everything through what she called the self-esteem test. If it made her feel good, it was a keeper. If not, it was "outta-there." After her experience with the sofa, Susan was happy to shed belongings that weakened her self-esteem and replace them with things that were life affirming. She replaced a chair that contained unhappy childhood memories and several pictures that depicted lonely-looking women.

The changes she made in her environment continued to reinforce her inner work. She joined a women's group dedicated to making peace with the past, kept a journal, and meditated every day. As time passed, confidence and self-love became Susan's constant companions, and she felt better than ever before.

One of your primary Feng Shui goals is to surround yourself with "environmental affirmations"—the things "who" are alive with life-affirming thoughts, feelings, memories, and associations. When you design your environment to reflect your ideal state of consciousness, you are opening the pathways for happiness, health, and prosperity to take up residence with you. With purpose and direction, you are setting your environmental stage to securely house your own personal state of grace.

### Feng Shui Principle II—Everything Is Connected by Ch'i

The second principle of Feng Shui is that every person, place, and thing is connected by Ch'i. The energy that connects us to our personal environment extends to include our entire planet. Energetically, there is no such thing as isolation. Although our connections are usually strongest with the people, places, and things that are close by, we are essentially in relationship with everyone and everything on Earth.

**<u>Our Connection with Ourselves and Other People:</u>** Unresolved conflict diminishes the quality of relationships. Because our culture believes that we can isolate ourselves from our own thoughts and feelings, as well as from each other, we don't always see the importance of resolving our inner and outer conflicts. Cultivating good relationships with self and others can seem insignificant. So what if you seethe every time your boss walks by, or you have objectionable neighbors, or you feel depressed when you look in the mirror. Your environment may include disagreeable clients, alienated family members, or troublesome co-workers. If you believe that you have no essential connection with the "problem" person or situation, you may not be motivated to improve the feelings you have about them. This changes dramatically when practicing Feng Shui. Negative reactions, feelings, and events that are supposedly small, but often repeated and left unresolved, accumulate, mar, and eventually scar, the quality of your life.

Practicing Feng Shui sometimes requires an attitude adjustment. Because we are essentially connected to every person, place, and thing, an important Feng Shui goal is to introduce healing thoughts, words, and deeds into every aspect of life. You may discover that your inner environment includes some negative points of view about yourself and others. All relationships—from your spouse to the grocery clerk—are vitally important. For better or worse, your connections with people—especially those people you are or were in regular contact with—ripple out and affect all aspects of your life. In recognizing the connection between relationships and quality of life, it is vital to practice generosity, compassion, honesty, and forgiveness with yourself and others.

When an elderly woman in my friend Adam's neighborhood was not able to keep up with her yard work, he decided to rake her leaves for her. Another neighbor noticed and came out to bag the leaves. A third neighbor joined them to prune the hedges. When the elderly woman noticed this trio of good Samaritans outside her window, she hurried to make refreshments for everyone. An hour later, the yard was beautiful, and everyone was inside having a tea party. Everyone in the whole neighborhood was strengthened by the generosity expressed in the simple neighborly act of caring for the yard of a person in need.

The opportunities to connect with each other in enriching ways are endless. Being cognizant of how connected you are to other people will give you the courage to heal old wounds, speak the truth, and have real heart-to-heart talks with relatives and friends. Likewise, treat yourself with more loving kindness, or perhaps, loving discipline. Make it a priority to do whatever you need to do to reinstate harmony and balance in all your relationships, knowing that the quality of your life depends on it.

**Our Connection with Our Belongings:** The quality of our relationships does not stop with people. We are also intimately connected to every single thing that surrounds us. The goal is to be conscious of everything we're connected to, which means *every thing* we own. If each of us only had five or six possessions, this wouldn't be an issue, but in our culture, most of us literally have thousands of possessions! To honor our connection with all these things, we need to let go of excess, and organize the rest. This includes all the stuff in the nooks and crannies we thought were "non-places," such as garages, basements, attics, closets, drawers, and cabinets. In Feng Shui, they all count.

Why take the time and go through the trouble to simplify and organize your belongings? Because they reflect your inner world and hold in place the conditions of your life. External order and harmony reflects internal order and harmony, while external clutter and chaos reflects internal clutter and chaos. This does not mean that you have to live a deprived existence—quite the opposite. Material well-being tends to increase in the presence of order. Let go of possessions that are unwanted and unneeded, and watch your inner clarity and outer opportunities blossom.

**The Many Facets of Our Lives:** Like a gemstone, every facet of your life is connected to all the others. You cannot separate your health from your finances, your finances from your relationships, or your relationships from your creativity. Therefore, the quality of each facet is equally important to the overall balance of life. An extremely stressful job takes a toll on relationships, physical vitality, and general outlook on life, even after five P.M. and on weekends. Our goal is to polish all of life's facets to equal brightness so that each one reflects the beauty of the other.

### Feng Shui Principle III— the Ch'i in Everything Is Always Changing

We witness change all the time in our bodies, relationships, energy level, state of mind, emotions, and in nature. The one constant in our physical universe is change. In Feng Shui, we accept change as a gift. We make friends with it. We embrace and invite change to continually make our lives *better*. So long as we are alive, we are growing and changing. When our homes reflect our changes, we move harmoniously forward.

Embracing change is often resisted in our culture. We are supposed to always look 25, buy furniture once, and choose one career we can stick with for a lifetime. As we all know, life doesn't work that way. Change happens. As we grow older and wiser, we may marry, have children, divorce, remarry, go back to school, change careers, move, make new friends—and through it all, experience tremendous inner and outer changes. When we are fully engaged in the dance of change and just let it happen, we are drawn to reinvent our homes to reflect our personal evolution.

**<u>Magic Moments of Change:</u>** From time to time, there are magic moments when you suddenly realize that something in your home really needs to change. You've changed, and now the house doesn't seem to reflect "you" anymore. In those moments, you are being summoned to update your environment to reflect and anchor your new inner program. Often these moments of clarity occur after you've been away from home for a while. You have a fresh perspective that acts like a spotlight, shedding light on things that are no longer useful or energizing in your space. *You've* changed—now your *environment* needs to change to embrace, support, and accurately reflect who you've become.

For instance, you may change careers and turn a guest room into a home office, or discover a new talent and transform the master bedroom into a dance studio. You take a trip down the Amazon or into the Himalayas, and when you return, you're different. As experiences along the way change you, it's vital to keep your inner and outer journey aligned. How you do this is completely up to you. You may feel compelled to paint your living room an earthy gold, bring the sound of water into your bedroom, create a meditation area, or remove existing art to display your Tibetan carvings or Colombian tapestries. When you feel the need to change something about your home, it's important to follow through as quickly as possible. In doing so, you embrace new ways of thinking, feeling, and acting, and you move forward in life.

I've witnessed this with clients. Many of them remark that when they've been away for a week, they are struck with an intense desire to change something about their environment when they return home. Their changes can be anything from a huge remodeling project to a small embellishment in one room. Clients with very little money can always find ways to change their homes with items that represent their inner journey—from a fresh flower in a vase, to a new candle or a collage made from the images found in a magazine. Whatever it is, the people who follow through and update their environments are following their instincts to align their homes with their inner growth and development. On the other hand, the people who see the need for change, but leave everything the way it is, often find that their homes and their lives become devitalized and stale. Ch'i is stimulated and nurtured by change. If we don't follow our instincts to change, eventually the vitality in our homes evaporates into thin air.

**Embracing Change:** Changing your living space anchors and supports the newest you, while the lack of change can keep old patterns in place. In our home, my husband, Brian, and I move our offices around occasionally to gain a fresh perspective on the world. My office "yells" at me when it's time for a change, and any change I make does not need to last forever. Feng Shui invites us all to lighten up about change, embrace it, and allow our environments to grow and move with us. Let the creative spark of your spirit run a little wild and enjoy the moment, knowing that change is your ally.

### Our New Foundation

Feng Shui observes that every person, place, and thing in our physical world is alive, interconnected, and always changing. We live in a dynamic world where everyone and everything matters and where every moment is unique. To bring the best out in ourselves, we create our homes to be our constant sources of inspiration and rejuvenation. In so doing, step by step, our homes become our personal paradises. I believe that this is our birthright if we choose to claim it.

Three practical guidelines borne out of the three foundational principles help us make choices and decisions that incorporate the timeless wisdom of Feng Shui.

### Practical Guideline I—Live with What You Love

One of the most powerful actions you can take is to live with what you love. The more you can do this, the better. Look through your Feng Shui eyes as you design, furnish, and arrange your home, and decide whether you truly love your choices. Save yourself from the plethora of poor designs by being thoughtful, creative, and downright picky. Choose what *you* love, even when it's not what a design magazine suggests. When you have to settle for or live with something you don't love, lift its energy by placing something nearby that makes your heart sing. For instance, I lived with a gray couch for a while that was not my favorite color. To make it work for me, I draped a beautiful cloth along the back. The deep reds and hand-painted details in the cloth harmonized with the sofa, and I lived happily with it until I could replace it with exactly what I wanted.

**Environmental Affirmations:** As you are sorting through your belongings, ask yourself, "Do I love this?" It's a great way to sort your possessions and decide "who" really belongs with you and "who" doesn't. Imagine for a moment being surrounded 100 percent by things that nourish, rejuvenate, and inspire you. In so doing, everything in your home becomes an Environmental Affirmation.

Obviously, this is a whole new way of seeing for many people. One of my clients almost fainted when she realized that she didn't love one thing in her house. Her home was functional and somewhat attractive, but did she love it? No! In this case, she began by bringing one object that she *did* love into her space. Like the red cloth I put on my gray couch, this began the process of moving the Ch'i toward excellence. Whether you begin with a flowering plant or comfortable new furniture, keep removing the unloved items and replacing them with those you love until you reach your goal. The more you practice living with what you love, the more exciting and affirmational your life will become.

**Sharing Space with Others:** What do you do when you live with others who don't share your taste in decor? Claim a room or nook that's all yours, and fill it with the things you love. Encourage those you live with to do the same. Couples and families with different tastes usually find it much easier to compromise in designing shared rooms when they each have an exclusive place or room they can call their own.

### *Practical Guideline II—Putting Safety and Comfort First*

Consider safety and comfort first when designing, furnishing, and arranging your home. Usually we consider beauty first, and if comfort or safety happens to be part of the package, that's a bonus. We see this in fashion—especially women's fashion. Women can look ravishing in formal gowns, for instance, and come close to suffocating or freezing, depending on the design. Add to the ensemble a stunning pair of high heels, and the misery is complete. Lovely to look at, yes; safe and comfortable, no! The basic needs of the body are often superseded by the desire to look beautiful.

Our singular focus on beauty is also found in the furniture industry.

Many people sit all day in lovely chairs that do not fit the contours of their bodies. When beautiful pieces of furniture have sharp corners or detailing, they don't pass the Feng Shui safety test. The prolific use of sharp angles in architecture can subvert our instinctual need for comfort and safety. Most of us have gotten so used to discomfort that we hardly notice it anymore. To make this point, I often ask audiences, "Who here has never sat in an uncomfortable chair?" Not one person has ever raised a hand. It is not unreasonable to demand comfort and safety. In fact, in Feng Shui, insisting on your environmental comfort and safety becomes crucial to the balance and harmony of your entire life. And as you design your home to be comfortable and safe, a new kind of beauty is born, turning your home into a deeply welcoming, healing, and sensual place to be.

**The Safety and Comfort Test:** Give your home a safety and comfort test. Look for sharp corners and detailing on your furniture and art that could injure shins, toes, and other body parts. I've visited homes where everyone in the family has been cut or bruised by furniture or architectural features that are as sharp as knives. What's amazing is that in most instances, it has never occurred to the family to do anything about these dangers—unless they're about to have a baby. To assure safety and comfort, baby-proof your home for people of all ages.

Safety in Feng Shui also addresses the placement of items in a room. Whenever possible, place furnishings such as beds and seating so that you can see the door from them. Please don't underestimate the power of locating yourself in the command position of a room. Even in the safest of circumstances, your nervous system relaxes more deeply when you have visual command of a room. This is often seen in the furniture arrangement of top executives. They wouldn't dream of sitting with their backs to the door! The viewless seats are for visitors and subordinates, while the executive maintains the power seat. As you place your furniture—including your bed, desk, sofas, and chairs—remember that sitting with a view of the door is the safest, most comfortable, and most powerful place in the room.

Feng Shui often addresses things that appear small and can be easily discounted or missed by the casual eye. Little things such as having your back to the door, bumping into sharp corners, or sitting in an uncomfortable chair add up; and like water dripping on a stone, they eventually make a permanent impression on your body, mind, and spirit.

### Practical Guideline III—Simplify and Organize

One of the greatest challenges in our abundant world is to simplify and organize our possessions. A colleague of mine swears that her belongings mate in the night, especially the ones in storage. Where there was one, a dozen now live. Crowded garages, basements, attics, and closets are often the showrooms of excess in our homes.

My family's attic was always a disaster area, since most things were thrown up there from the bottom of the stairs. As a result, it was extremely annoying to climb those stairs and try to find anything. I can still remember my father's language as he banged around overhead looking for the right suitcase. Our basement was a virtual indoor dumpster/hardware store, where I would sweat bullets looking for the tool Dad sent me to find. I had a perfect track record: I never once found what he wanted. Our house ate scissors and keys, while every drawer in the house had everything in it, except what I needed at the time.

So, when I began to practice Feng Shui, I had to learn some new skills—how to simplify and thoroughly organize my possessions. I found all forms of clutter in my space, including piles of papers, drawers of ragged clothes, and shelves of old china and linens—things that I didn't love or want and hadn't used for a long time. I kept all that stuff around because I didn't realize that my vast collection of unwanted stuff was congesting the flow of vital energy throughout my life.

As I cleared the stuff out, I noticed a rather magical thing happening: The more I released the old, the more I received the new—in the form of wonderful new belongings and opportunities that I really *did* want and need. I'd simplify and organize my closet, give away a bag of clothes, and the next thing I knew, I'd find the perfect *new* clothes. Then, I'd be invited to an event, wear my new clothes, meet people interested in my work, and my business would expand. I'd sort through my cabinets, get rid of things I no longer had a use for, and something I needed or wanted to do would soon flow into my life. It's absolutely predictable.

**Active Chaos—Creativity in Motion:** Chaos is part of the spice of life. Flurries of creative activity, with all their attendant mess, happen every day. It is the natural and necessary spilling out of materials to create a new masterpiece. It's seen in the paints and brushes that are scattered around the painter, the reference books that pile up around a writer, and the jars and pots that encircle a cook. You know when chaos is active when you are attracted to it. Something—a painting, a book, a meal—is being born! You sense the dynamic nature of creativity, and you want to taste it, smell it, see it, and revel in its aliveness. Whether it's a new project, a new sauce, or a new garden, active chaos generates excitement. The key to keeping excitement and creativity alive is to "stay in the loop" and reorganize the space and materials between creative bursts.

**Passive Chaos—Creativity Lost in Clutter:** Chaos left for long becomes passive or stagnant, and the scene changes. No masterpiece is born in a studio filled with dried-up brushes and spilled paints, nor in a kitchen full of crusty dishes and greasy pans. The longer we leave "the mess," the more the Ch'i deteriorates, and the flurry of creation grinds to a halt. Creativity languishes on the cluttered desktop, in the chaotic kitchen, and on the junky back porch. Even when your rooms are free of passive chaos, check your storage areas. There, the kingdom of passive chaos might include mountains of catalogs, cities of rusty old paint cans, or forests of toys the kids outgrew a dozen years ago. Thickets of passive chaos grow in garages, closets, basements, and attics, safely behind closed doors. Feng Shui invites you to throw open all the doors and take a look. Passive chaos is easy to recognize. In its presence, creativity collapses, and there's no reviving it until that big, old mess is handled. Behind a door or not, clutter and chaos drain your vitality. That's why it's often so challenging to face the mess and return it to order. Nevertheless, it has to be done. It's helpful to realize that as you bravely roust the minions of passive chaos from your home, you are inviting transformation to occur. You are bringing your creativity and imagination back to life.

Here are seven questions to ask while sorting through your possessions that can help you clear the passive chaos and establish a new order.

### Seven "Clear the Way" Questions

1. Do I love it?
2. Do I need it?
3. Does it support who I am now in my life?
4. Does it act as an Environmental Affirmation for me?
5. What positive and/or negative thoughts, memories, or emotions do I associate with it?
6. Does it need to be fixed or repaired, and am I willing to do so now?
7. If it's time to let it go, am I going to sell, lend, or give it away, and when?

**Eliminate Passive Chaos and Reclaim Creativity:** Organizing your possessions reinstates your creativity and vitality. Motivation kicks in when you understand the importance of cleaning up the chaotic spots in your home. As you simplify and organize, watch what happens in your life. Since everything is connected, the simple act of cleaning out a drawer can ripple out and attract positive opportunities. If you feel overwhelmed, ask for a friend or family member's support. If you're just too busy, hire a professional organizer to help you. However you accomplish the task, your reward is a ticket to enter (or re-enter) the dynamic world of creativity and the active chaos that goes with it. Active chaos is an integral part of the creative cycle. The trick is to follow the natural cycle all the way around and bring your projects to completion. Enjoy the ride from beginning to end, knowing that your creative expression renews the spirit, nurtures the home, and enhances every facet of your life.

### Practice Feng Shui Today

The best time to practice Feng Shui is today. Waiting for the perfect conditions is like waiting to begin exercising or to start eating well. The energy that moves through your home is of vital importance to your health, prosperity, and happiness *now*. So begin designing your perfect home—your personal paradise—today, wherever you are. When it comes right down to it, you are renting, whether you own your home or not. Don't let plans to move keep you from making the home you live in now the best it can be. Balancing and enhancing your present home is one of the most powerful things you can do to energize and manifest your goals and dreams for the future.

Feng Shui principles give you an abundance of practical, results-producing ways to balance and improve your life. Begin by joining forces with your home. Set your intentions for positive change with clarity and purpose. Then take action. Explore your connection with the things "who" surround you. Simplify and organize every nook and cranny so that your creative spirit has room to flourish. Embrace change, live with what you love, and let comfort and safety be your guides. As each of us embraces these principles, together we'll create Heaven on Earth.

*Chapter Two*

# THE BAGUA MAP—
# CALLING ALL BLESSINGS

*"The pleasure of the soul appears to be found in the
journey of discovery, the unfolding revelation of
expanded insight and experience."*
— Anthony Lawlor

One of the most results-producing tools in Feng Shui is the Bagua Map. By correlating the structure and design of your home with the blessings of vitality, happiness, and good fortune, the Bagua Map shows you how to summon positive change into your life. When you seriously embrace the directives of the Bagua Map, obstacles fall away, powerful changes occur, and blessings manifest. To work with the Bagua Map is to stand in the presence of your own destiny and say, "I am ready."

**FIGURE 2A**

*The Bagua Map*

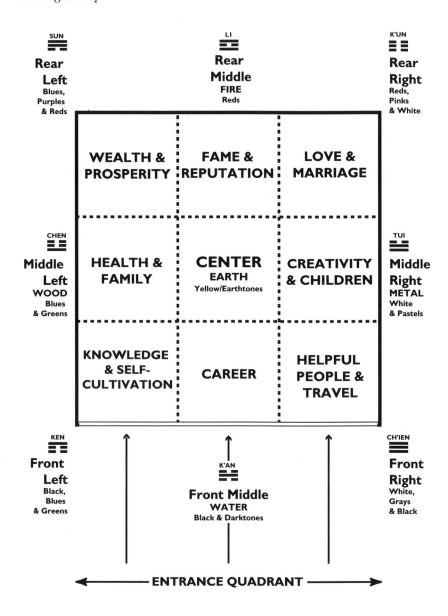

The word *Bagua* literally means "eight trigrams." These trigrams form the basic building blocks of the *I Ching* (the Chinese Book of Changes) and are each associated with (among other things) blessings such as health, wealth, love, and creativity. The Bagua Map, or map of the eight trigrams, charts where each of these blessings is located in your home. You find that the good fortune you cherish—or aspire to—is being energized or depleted in your living room, bedroom, garage, and closets. What were two completely separate aspects of life—your home and your "luck"—merge into one powerful highway that leads to positive change and lasting blessings.

People have solved many problems using the Bagua Map. It's uncanny how often people find a correlation between the way their homes are designed and their ongoing problems. One couple found that the Wealth and Prosperity area of their home was located in a bathroom with leaky plumbing, symbolic of the continual leaking away of their savings account. Another couple discovered that the Career area of their home was located in the garage, which was crammed with junk, a perfect metaphor for the stagnant condition of their professional lives. A single woman discovered that her Love and Marriage area was located on a back porch full of empty pots and dead plants—symbols of her empty, dead love life.

Ultimately, the Bagua Map leads you to the discovery that all parts of your home and your life are of equal importance. Every area within and without needs to be well maintained; clutter-free; and arranged to flow with ease, beauty, and grace. To embrace Feng Shui to its fullest, focus on the corresponding inner work while improving and enhancing your home. Do some soul-searching. Make some inner "home improvements." When you work with the Bagua Map in this way, you create a flow of vital energy in yourself and in your home. This, in turn, produces the most deeply satisfying and long-lasting results, and attracts blessings into every facet of your life.

## *Mapping the Bagua of Your Home*

### FIGURE 2B

*To make your Bagua map, you need a blueprint or footprint drawing of your home.*

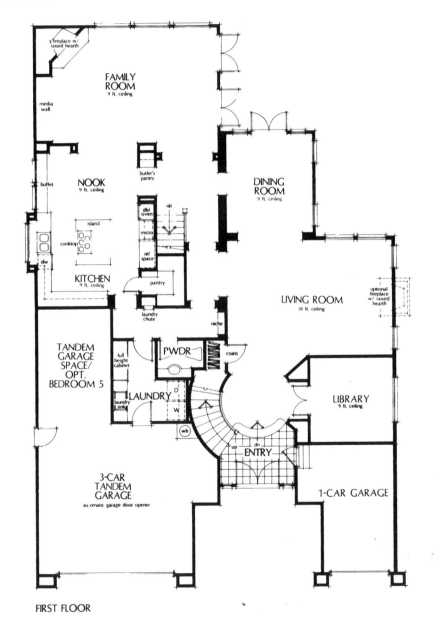

FIRST FLOOR

**FIGURE 2C**

*Divide your drawing into nine equal areas, like a tic-tac-toe board, and label*
*each area as shown here and in Figure 2A.*

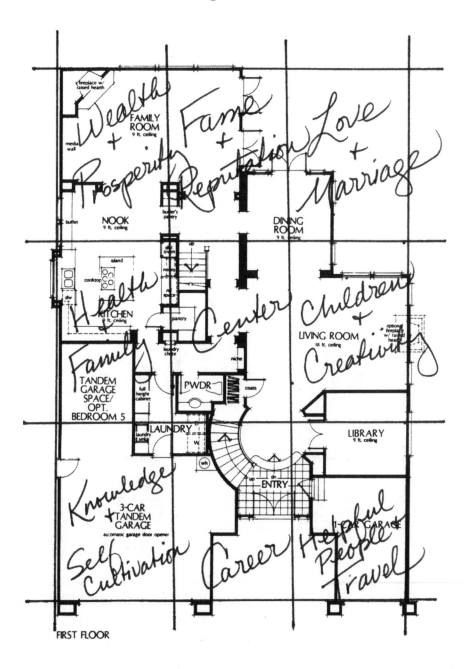

**FIGURE 2D**

*Translate the Bagua Map of the main floor directly to upper and lower floors, like second stories, attics, or basements, and enhance accordingly.*

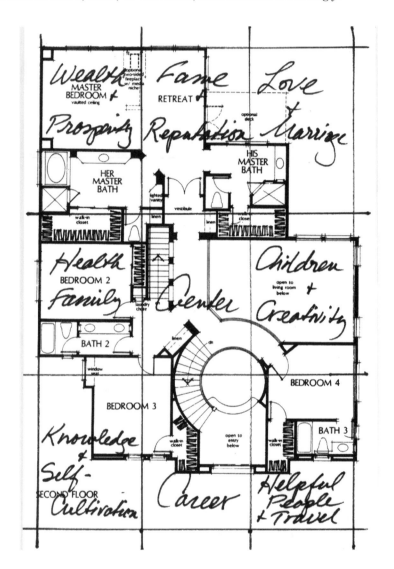

### Mapping the Bagua

The Bagua Map can be applied to any fixed shape—including buildings, rooms, and furniture. These instructions are geared toward mapping your home, and once you understand the basics, you can map any structure. You will need a bird's-eye drawing of your home, such as the blueprint or footprint sketch shown in Figure 2B. Determine the overall shape of your home by including all parts that are attached to it—such as garages, porches, room additions, arbors, storage huts, and decks with railings.

Lay the drawing down (as you see in Figure 2B) so that the front entrance of your home is at the bottom of the page. Now, draw a rectangle around your home just big enough to include every part of the home inside it, as shown in Figure 2C. This is the outline of your Bagua Map. Divide the outline into nine even sections, like a tic-tac-toe board, and label the nine squares as shown in Figures 2A and 2C. This is your complete Bagua Map.

When your home is a simple rectangle (Figure 2E), you will find that all of the Bagua areas are located inside the structure of your house. If your home is any other shape, such as an L, S, T, or U, you'll find areas located within the rectangular outline of the Bagua Map, but outside the structure of your house. Whether indoors or outdoors, it's very important to determine each *"Gua's,"* or area's, location. For instance, the home in Figures 2B, 2C, and 2D is missing much of the Love and Marriage area, as well as some of the Career, and Helpful People and Travel, areas.

**FIGURE 2E**

*This basic sketch of a rectangular home, with its front entrance located in the Knowledge and Self-Cultivation area of the Bagua Map, has all the Bagua areas contained in the physical structure of the house.*

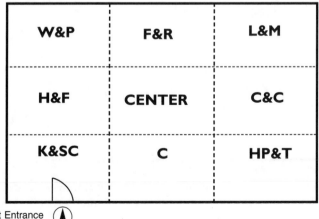

Front Entrance

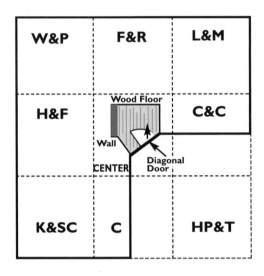

**FIGURE 2F**

*This is a sketch of a home with a diagonal door. The foyer wall, floor covering, and direction in which the door opens help determine which way to map the house.*

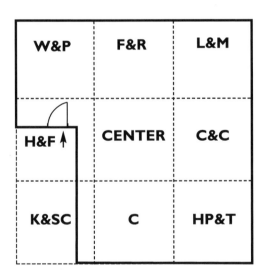

**FIGURE 2G**

*This recessed front door is located in the Health and Family area of this home's Bagua Map. Notice that a portion of Health and Family, and Knowledge and Self-Cultivation, are outside the home's structure.*

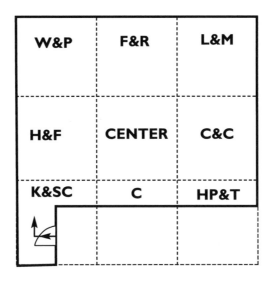

| W&P | F&R | L&M |
|-----|-----|-----|
| H&F | CENTER | C&C |
| K&SC | C | HP&T |

**FIGURE 2H**

*When a front door is recessed to the very back of the house, the Bagua Map is turned to fit over the main body of the house, as seen here. Notice that part of Knowlege and Self-Cultivation, Career, and Helpful People and Travel are missing from the structure of the house.*

### CLARIFYING POINTS

1.  Don't be concerned about where the walls are located inside the house. As you can see in Figure 2C, sometimes one large room will subdivide into two or three Bagua areas, or one area might encompass two or three small rooms.

2.  If your home has more than one story, partial or full, translate the Bagua Map of the main floor directly up or down to other levels, as shown in Figure 2D. Multiple floors give you multiple opportunities to enhance certain Bagua areas in your home, but you only have to be concerned with completing the main floor.

3.  When your front door is built on a diagonal, use walls, flooring, or the direction you see first when you open the front door to determine which way to map the house, as shown in Figure 2F.

4.  When your front door is recessed past the front wall of the house, you may be entering your home through the Health and Family, Center, or Children and Creativity areas of the Bagua Map, as in Figure 2G. If your front door is recessed to the very back, turn the Bagua Map to fit over the main body of the house, as shown in Figure 2H.

5.  Because the home is larger than each room, it holds more Ch'i. Therefore, work first with the Bagua Map of the home, and then with each room.

6.  Consult a Feng Shui practitioner if you need help making a Bagua Map of your home. (See the back of the book in order to locate a practitioner near you.)

### *Missing Areas of the Bagua Map*

When there are Bagua areas outside the physical structure of your home, it's important to define and enhance them in some way. This can be as simple as installing an outdoor lamppost, ornamental tree, or large statue where the corner would be if the structure were rectangular. Enhancements such as flagpoles, large boulders, trees, fences, water features, and outdoor sculptures can be grouped to enhance the area and increase the Ch'i flow in and around your home. Filling in a Gua can also be done by adding a deck, patio, arbor, or room addition. The goal is to anchor or complete the missing area with something significant that's in harmony with your home, as shown in Figures 2I and 2J.

**FIGURE 2I**

*This is a view of the home's Love and Marriage area, a footprint drawing of which appears in Figure 2B, taken shortly after the new owners moved in.* ***(Also in color, page 113.)***

**FIGURE 2J**

*To anchor the Love and Marriage area, the couple chose to plant an olive tree, symbolizing strength and longevity of love. A large built-in planter and flower border further accent the area. They also added outdoor living areas to both floors, enhancing the beauty and functionality of the Love and Marriage area.* ***(Also in color, page 113.)***

## *Personalizing Your Choices*

Whenever you can, choose items and designs that relate to the Bagua area you are working with. As seen in Figure 2J, an olive tree was chosen to represent the strength and longevity of the couple's love for each other, while the planter adds structure; and the flowers, beauty and color. Both outdoor living areas include intimate seating for two. Their Career area, shown in Figure 5C on page 97, shows the large fountain they chose in order to enhance their professional lives. There is no end to the creative possibilities you can draw from as you anchor the Bagua areas found outside the structure of your home.

**When You Can't Do Anything Outside:** Don't be discouraged if you can't do anything substantial to enhance the Bagua on the outside of your home. There are still many ways you can symbolically complete a missing Gua.

**Symbolic Enhancements:** Missing Bagua areas can be completed energetically by "planting" a natural quartz crystal (or other meaningful object) where the corner of the house would be if it were a rectangle (Figure 2K). Bury the crystal, point up, an inch or two in the ground, with the intention of lifting and strengthening the Ch'i. Your intention coupled with the crystal strengthens and supports the area that is missing in structure. If pavement covers the missing area, use paint instead of a crystal to mark the spot. Be as subtle or as creative as you'd like, knowing that your intention to positively influence the flow of Ch'i combined with the physical act of marking the spot makes your enhancement powerful.

## Figure 2K

*When you cannot do anything "big" outside, find the missing corner and bury a natural quartz crystal (or other meaningful object) pointed up an inch or two in the ground, with the intention of energizing the area. Another idea is to paint pavement with a circle or line to mark the spot. Work from the inside by hanging a mirror or art with depth on the wall closest to the missing area. Or use plants, flowers, water fountains, crystals, or personal Ch'i enhancements to build and increase the energy in the area.*

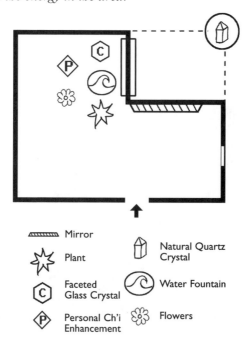

- ⎯⎯⎯ Mirror
- ✹ Plant
- Ⓒ Faceted Glass Crystal
- ⓟ Personal Ch'i Enhancement
- ⬡ Natural Quartz Crystal
- ◯ Water Fountain
- ❀ Flowers

Indoors, hang a mirror or art with depth on the wall closest to the missing area. This symbolically opens up the space to include what's missing. Or, use any of the Ch'i enhancements (Chapter 4) to power up the windows and walls located near missing Guas. It's also very important to pay special attention to improving and enhancing the Bagua area in each room that's missing in your home's structure. Many times, the same area that's missing in the home's structure is also challenging in each room. For instance, a home that is missing the Wealth and Prosperity area often has cluttered closets, unhealthy plants, and disliked possessions located in the Wealth and Prosperity areas of every room in the house. Make sure nothing in your home is holding an unfortunate situation in place.

## *Mapping the Bagua in Every Room*

### Figure 2L

*The bedroom, along with being in the Health and Family area of the house (shown in Figure 2D), has its own Bagua Map. Each room will have its own Map, which may or may not correspond to the home's overall Bagua Map.*

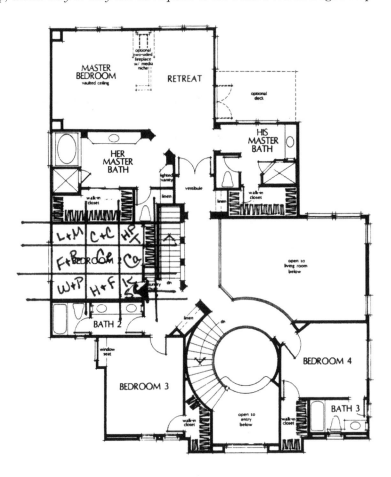

Follow the same steps when mapping a room that you used when mapping your home. Draw the footprint of the room, place the main door into the room at the bottom of the page, draw a rectangle around the perimeter, divide it into nine equal parts, and label each section according to the Bagua Map. If there is more than one entrance into a room, choose the one that's used most often. Or if they seem to be used equally, choose one of the doors as the entrance for mapping the Bagua of the room.

Please note that the Bagua of your home and of each room often *won't* coincide. The door or entry into a space is your guide when making a Bagua Map, and each room can be individually mapped and enhanced accordingly. For instance, Figure 2L shows a bedroom located in the Health and Family area of the house's Bagua Map. But, as you can see, it also has its own room-sized Map. So, take both the house and room Maps into consideration when decorating the space. If the room is used as a home office, it could be furnished in wood to enhance its Health and Family placement in the house's Bagua Map. If that same room is used as a bedroom, it could be given a garden or floral theme. The room's placement in the Health and Family area of the home's Bagua Map also makes it an excellent place for massage, yoga, or exercise. Then, depending on its function, the placement of furnishings and decor within the room can be guided by the room's Bagua Map.

In Figure 2L, the room functions as the husband's office. With an eye on his home's Bagua Map, he chose a wooden desk, credenza, and filing cabinets as his office furniture. Then he turned to the *room's* Bagua Map. He placed his desk in the Children and Creativity area of the room, which enhances his resourcefulness and affords him a commanding view of door and window. The closet in the Helpful People and Travel and Career areas is fitted with shelves for his office supplies and equipment. Across from his desk, family photos are hung over the credenza in the room's Health and Family area. A recent photo of him and his wife sits on the filing cabinet in the Love and Marriage area, while an arrangement of plants and a sculptural water feature fill Wealth and Prosperity. Here, in his "powerhouse of productivity," his business thrives.

### Assessing Your Bagua Map Profile

Take a good look at each Bagua area of your home, then of each room, and answer the following questions:

- What room or area is located in each Bagua area?

- What possessions are located there?
- Are they organized?
- Do I love everything I see?
- Do I see a correlation between what's located in each area and the quality of my life?
- What can I improve?
- What is the first area I'm going to work with?

This can be a very revealing process! We often find that the condition of the Bagua areas in our homes has a direct correlation with that particular facet of our lives. Consider the woman whose only complaint was that she still smoked cigarettes. Flourishing in her Health and Family area was a pencil cactus growing in sections the length and width of a cigarette. In the cactus's decorative planter was a beautiful red wooden carving of a flame.

Or how about the woman whose main concern was that her husband worked very long hours and she was often alone? In their Love and Marriage area, located in the master bedroom, was a painting of a forlorn-looking woman, alone and hunched over a café table, in the eternal posture of waiting. Both husband and wife viewed this painting from their bed—a constant anchor and reminder of the tension in their marriage.

This happens all the time. The objects we surround ourselves with on a daily basis are either nurturing us or they're not. If they're not, they may be holding unfortunate situations in place. Once removed, the Ch'i improves. When the first woman replaced the cactus with the environmentally affirming vase of fragrant flowers, she was able to quit smoking. Instead of smoke, she filled her nose and lungs with the scent of roses and freesias. The second woman removed the sad art that was holding court in the bedroom and replaced it with a romantic picture of two people having a picnic. Soon her loneliness was replaced by frequent lunch and dinner dates with her husband during the week.

There are also times when it's not that simple. When you want to change something in your life that is mediocre, unhappy, or stressful, you may experience some chaos as a new order is being established. For instance, if you are unhappy in your marriage and decide to enhance the Love and Marriage Gua to reinstate marital bliss, the first thing you'll be faced with are the reasons why you're unhappy. Working with the Bagua enhances the flow of Ch'i, and the enhanced flow will push whatever is hidden out into the open. If you aspire to excellence, everything mediocre has to be cleared away first.

Recently, I worked with a woman named Nan who felt very stuck in life. Her tiny apartment had neither a bathtub nor a real kitchen, frustrating her desires for leisurely bathing and gourmet cooking. The yoga classes she taught remained small, despite all her efforts to attract larger groups. She was very clear about what she wanted: a bigger home with a proper kitchen and bathtub, and larger classes filled with serious yoga students.

When mapping the Bagua of her townhouse, we found that the Helpful People and Travel and Career areas were located in a sad little patch of bare ground near her front door. Nan amended the soil, planted flowers and ferns, and accented the area with a statue of St. Francis to symbolize "helpful people." She also took a look at her feelings about success, and realized that being small was comfortable because it was familiar. To get bigger, she was going to have to relate to success in a new way.

Three days later, Nan received a notice from her landlord giving her 30 days to vacate so that he could move in. Simultaneously, she received enough student sign-ups to require a larger room for classes. The Ch'i was moving, and rather than feeling stuck, she was feeling quite stimulated. The sudden changes required tremendous focus and trust on her part. As she went through the steps of finding another home and classroom, the familiarity of staying "small and miserable" transformed. Six weeks later, Nan was teaching in a lovely new studio and living in a "heavenly" place—a spacious one-bedroom cottage that had been specifically built for a person who was exactly her height! The kitchen was bright and roomy, and the bathtub was divine.

Bringing this ancient wisdom into your household can feel like a whirlwind at first, as your intentions find their way into physical form. Life can become downright chaotic as parts of it are rearranged to harmoniously reflect your goals. Map the sea of Ch'i that flows through your home, and shape it to reflect who you are now and all that you are aspiring to be. And get ready. It's my experience that your call for positive change is always answered.

## *The Inner and Outer Work Related to the Bagua Map*

As you work with the Bagua Map, take the time to complement your outer efforts with personal inner development. Contemplate how you can improve your character (the unseen) as you surround yourself with improvements and enhancements (the seen) that you *love*; don't settle for less! The more you personalize your choices, the better. Remember, your incorporation of inner and outer work produces the most deeply satisfying and long-lasting results.

### Inner Work Related to Health and Family

Key Word: *Strength*

The blessings of Health and Family are associated with the *I Ching* trigram *Chen,* translated as "Shocking Thunder." Unexpected shocks or sudden unforeseen problems cycle through our lives like stormy weather. Just as we need our homes to be in good repair to weather a storm, we need to be in good repair ourselves. To do this, we need to cultivate the two vital attributes that strengthen physical vitality and emotional health: honesty and forgiveness.

Your ability to be completely honest maintains healthy boundaries— boundaries that include knowing when a meal, person, place, or situation is healthy for you or not. When you can respond honestly to life's many temptations, you have the power to clearly say yes or no. Honesty demands that you give a truthful answer, then forgiveness directs you to let it go. Forgiveness is your ticket to staying in the power position of the present moment. Your sense of physical and emotional strength and well-being thrives on moving forward without heavy baggage. Honesty and forgiveness keep your vitality and your relationships strong. According to the *I Ching,* this assures good fortune and the strength to survive all challenges.

Assess your exercise, sleeping, and eating habits, and determine how well you are maintaining your body. Strengthen your physical and emotional health by sending family and friends loving thoughts every time you think of them. Be honest with yourself and others in a loving way. Forgive everyone you feel has ever harmed or hurt you. Let them go. Most important, forgive yourself. The past is over, and the present is a clean page ready to become your masterpiece. Affirm: *"I am strong and vibrant in body, heart, mind, and spirit. I completely forgive myself and others for past occurrences, and send loving, healing thoughts to all my relations. I enjoy a healthy, honest, loving relationship with myself and every friend and family member."*

### Enhance the Health and Family area of your home when:

- your health needs a boost.
- you are planning or recovering from a medical procedure.
- you are beginning or already participating in sports, dance, or exercise.
- you would like your social life and your "family of choice" to grow or improve.
- you would like your relationship with relatives to improve.
- you want to strengthen the attributes of honesty and forgiveness.

### Outer enhancements related to Health and Family:

- Healthy plants with rounded leaves or a soft, graceful appearance
- Fresh flowers
- Dried and silk flowers and plants with a fresh, vibrant appearance
- Artwork depicting your concept of ideal health
- Posters and paintings of gardens and landscapes
- Floral prints and stripes, including linens, wallpaper, and upholstery
- Anything made from wood, such as tables, chairs, bowls, and vases
- Pillars, columns, and pedestals
- Photos of family and friends
- Blues and greens
- Quotes, sayings, and affirmations concerning honesty and forgiveness

### Inner Work Related to Wealth and Prosperity

Key Word: *Gratitude*

Translated as "Persistent Wind," the *I Ching* trigram *Sun* is related to Wealth and Prosperity. In most cases, your wealth is accumulated over time, much as a tree is shaped by prevailing winds. To fully appreciate the magnitude of your wealth, cultivate an attitude of gratitude. Money is only one small part of your wealth and prosperity. You shape your life with all that you hold dear—from your close friends, family, and health, to your own burgeoning wisdom and talents. And, as with money, it is wise not to gamble with, or take for granted, the many gifts in life that make up your riches. The key to gathering and multiplying wealth is to persist in seeing the half-full glass.

Wealth gathers in a grateful pocket. Make a list of all the people and things you are grateful for each day. Add to the list all the qualities and talents you are blessed with. You now have a complete accounting of your wealth and prosperity. Notice how rich you are at this moment. As you focus on being grateful, aspects of your life keep revealing themselves, adding to your portfolio. Gratitude is your pathway to the steadfast experience of wealth and prosperity on every level. Read your list often, add to it, and revel in just how rich you really are. Affirm: *"With joy and gratitude, I welcome an abundance of positive people and experiences into my life, now and always. I am rich and prosperous in every way, and blessed with a constant and abundant flow of health, wealth, and happiness."* Build your portfolio of wealth with gratitude, and your prosperity is assured.

#### *Enhance the Wealth and Prosperity area of your home when:*

- you want to generate more cash flow in your life.
- you're raising money or resources for a special purpose.
- you'd like to feel more grateful for the flow of abundance and prosperity in your life.

#### *Outer enhancements related to Wealth and Prosperity:*

- Water features, especially when the water is moving

- Wind chimes, prayer flags, and banners that symbolically call in wealth and prosperity

- Beloved possessions and collections that are literally valuable, such as antiques, art, crystal, and coins

- Posters, paintings, and photographs of the things you'd like to buy or experience

- All blues, purples, and reds

- Sayings, quotes, and affirmations related to gratitude, wealth, and prosperity

### Inner Work Related to Fame and Reputation

Key Word: *Integrity*

The *I Ching* trigram *Li,* representing Fame and Reputation, means "Clinging Fire." Like fire, your reputation has a way of clinging to you for a long time. A good reputation, earned by the steadfast practice of integrity, inspires good will and fans the flames for great things to happen. Bridges to good fortune can only be built in the clear light of integrity. On the other hand, insincerity and dishonesty can burn your bridges. Your words and actions are remembered, and often exaggerated, long after they've been said and done. Be mindful of what you are famous for—it will cling to you for a long time.

This is true whether or not anyone else knows about your miscue. The one person you want to establish an impeccable reputation with most is *yourself.* When you are accountable in thought, word, and deed, you illuminate your path through life. Evaluate your level of integrity. Do you consider yourself a person of sound character? Do you keep your word? Only you know how truly honest—or not—you really are. Let any act of insincerity or dishonesty become a thing of the past, and practice "being your word." It is your integrity that builds and strengthens your reputation, and cultivates the priceless rewards of self-respect and self-esteem. Affirm: *"My integrity inspires good will and good fortune. I am trustworthy in all that I say and do."*

### *Enhance the Fame and Reputation area of your home when:*

- you want to establish a good reputation in your community.

- you would like more recognition at work or at home.

- you'd like to be well known for something you do.
- you want to raise your level of integrity.

### *Outer enhancements related to Fame and Reputation:*

- Symbols of your accomplishments, such as diplomas, awards, certificates, or trophies
- Pleasant lighting
- Artwork that depicts people or animals
- Items that are made from animals, such as leather, faux fur, feathers, bone, and wool
- Images of people you respect
- Symbols of your goals for the future
- Objects or patterns that are triangular or conical in shape
- All subtle, bright, and deep shades of red
- Sayings, quotes, and affirmations relating to integrity, and to your fame and reputation

## Inner Work Related to Love and Marriage

Key Word: *Receptivity*

Love and Marriage are related to the *I Ching* Trigram *K'un,* or "Receptive Earth." As the most Yin of all the trigrams, this teaching encourages the cultivation of receptivity and unconditional love. To truly receive love, you must open your heart and be entirely receptive to your partner. The armor falls in the presence of *amore.* Successful intimate love relationships thrive when *both* partners trust each other completely and give and receive from each other with open hearts. All happy couples know how mushy, soft, gentle, loving, and sweet they can be in their intimate moments together. These are all Yin qualities, and they make the difference between an ordinary and an extraordinary love life.

Perhaps the most important love life you can cultivate is the one with yourself. Treat yourself with the same tender loving care you would a lover. Be open to lovingly fulfilling your own needs, wishes, and aspirations. Your ability to love yourself enhances your Ch'i and attracts loving people to you. Take yourself on dates to places you love, soak in a hot bath, light candles, and play your favorite music. Allow your own deepest rhythms to emerge and be celebrated. Practice openly giving and receiving love from the one person you will know most intimately for a lifetime—yourself. Look in the mirror and say: *"You are a magnificent person. I love and support you completely, now and always."*

### *Enhance the Love and Marriage area of your home when:*

- you would like to attract a romantic relationship.
- you want to improve the romantic relationship you have now.
- you are developing or enriching a loving relationship with yourself.
- you want to be more open-hearted and receptive.

### *Outer enhancements related to Love and Marriage:*

- Artwork portraying romance and love
- Pairs of things, such as candlesticks, flowers, books, and statues
- Mementos from romantic experiences
- Favorite photographs of you, or you and your true love
- Items in reds, pinks, and white
- Quotes, sayings, and affirmations on love and romance

## Inner Work Related to Children and Creativity

Key Word: *Joy*

The *I Ching* trigram *Tui,* meaning "Joyous Lake," is associated with Children and Creativity and the attributes of joy and encouragement. We are all creators in life. You are constantly creating something, whether it's new cells in your body, new thoughts in your mind, new meals in the kitchen, or new projects at work. To live is to create, and to create is to be truly alive. The key to entering fully into the creative process is joy. The joy and pleasure you take in your everyday creations connects you with the joy of all creation. A child's natural ability to spontaneously create art, plays, songs, poems, dances, skits, games, and music erupts from the joy of being alive. It is the pure childlike quality of joy within us all that carries the creative spirit.

Take every opportunity to encourage creativity. Spend time with creative people, go to art galleries, make collages that express your goals and dreams, buy a box of crayons or colored pencils, and let your creative spirit flow. Nurture yourself and others with large helpings of encouragement so that creativity flourishes all around you. Let children and adults alike know how wonderful their creative works are, even when their sky is orange, their chimneys are crooked, their trees look like lollipops, or their people have three arms. In the spirit of joyful creativity, it's perfect! The *I Ching* suggests that when you encourage the creativity in people to come out and play, you enlighten the world with joy.

Think of some of the creative experiences you've had. In the best of all possible worlds, your creativity was supported and encouraged every step of the way by an enthusiastic fan club of friends, family, and mentors who said, "Wow, good work!" and "That's so beautiful!" If not, you may have felt vulnerable and discouraged when your creative work was met with "What an awful color!" "It's not the right shape!" or "It needs salt." Whether you have been encouraged to be creative or not, take stock of your daily creative expressions. Whether it's dressing imaginatively or telling stories to your children, any action can be creative, depending on how you approach it.

Step into being the enthusiastic creator of harmony, health, and beauty in your environment. Stimulate your creative juices by doing things that really turn you on. Awaken your creative genius by letting your inner child come out and play. Turn the music up in your living room, and move to the beat. Sing at the top of your lungs in the car. Get good and dirty in the garden. Do as much of what fills you with joy as possible.

Ultimately, you are your own greatest fan. Nurture your inner environment with joy, encouragement, and delight. Repeat affirmations such as: *"I experience great joy and pleasure in creatively expressing myself. I attract joyful, fun people who encourage me to be creative. The more I express myself creatively, the happier I am."*

### *Enhance the Children and Creativity area of your home when:*

- you want to be more creative in any way.
- you are involved in a creative project.
- you feel creatively blocked.
- you want to explore and develop your inner-child qualities.

- you'd like to improve your relationship with children.
- you would like to become pregnant.
- you want to experience more joy.

### Outer enhancements related to Children and Creativity:

- Art or objects that are especially creative, whimsical, playful, colorful, or that stimulate your creative juices
- Toys, dolls, and stuffed animals that bring you joy
- Photographs of children, along with anything children have made by hand
- Rocks and stones
- Circular and oval shapes
- Items made from metal
- Items in white or light pastels
- Quotes, sayings, and affirmations that apply to joy, children, and creativity

## Inner Work Related to Helpful People and Travel

Key Word: *Synchronicity*

The Helpful People and Travel area is associated with the *I Ching* trigram *Ch'ien,* meaning "Heaven." This is the most Yang of the trigrams, and is associated with clarity, synchronicity, and right action. You create "Heaven on Earth" when you focus clearly on what you want to accomplish, and then take action accordingly, letting synchronicity be your guide. Think of a time when your life was positively changed by a helpful person or special place. Perhaps you met someone who became your mentor, or you were traveling in a place that enriched your life. Touched by the experience of synchronicity, you found yourself in the right place, meeting the right people, at just the right time. When you experience the people in your life as angels, and the places where you live, work, and play as paradises, you're "in sync." The opposite experience, replete with its devilish people and punishing places, clearly tells you that you need to reset your path. You know you're back on track when the angelic people and heavenly experiences reappear like signposts showing the way.

Cultivate clarity of mind, heart, and spirit; set your intentions; focus upon them; say no to what doesn't match, and yes to what does. In this way, heavenly moments expand into hours, days, weeks—a lifetime.

As with all powerful experiences, transforming your present world takes tremendous focus and action. Decide to be your own angel. Create your own heavenly place. Let synchronicity be your guide. Affirm: *"I attract the perfect people, places, and things into my life every day. I am always in the right place and meeting the right people at the right time. Calling all angels: I welcome you into my life!"*

### Enhance the Helpful People and Travel area of your home when:

- you want to attract more mentors, clients, customers, employees, colleagues—helpful people of any description—into your life.
- you want to travel in general, or to a particular place.
- you would like to feel more connected to your spiritual or religious belief system—the ultimate "helpful people."
- you are moving to a new home or work location.
- you want to experience more synchronicity.

### Outer enhancements related to Helpful People and Travel:

- Art that depicts religious or spiritual figures you love, such as angels, saints, goddesses, and teachers
- Objects that have personal spiritual associations, such as a rosary, crystal, or book of prayers
- Photographs of people who have been helpful to you, such as mentors, teachers, or relatives
- Art, posters, and collages of places you'd like to visit or live, or that are special to you
- Items in white, gray, and black
- Quotes, sayings, and affirmations on miracles, heavenly experiences, and synchronicity

### Inner Work Related to Career

Key Word: *Courage*

The *I Ching* trigram associated with your life's work or career is *K'an,* meaning "Deep Water." Many of us know how unsettling it can be to decide on a career path. Like it or not, we are swept into our own depths as we explore a potential vocation. Once chosen, the path can be mysterious, often leading to unforeseen challenges, and yes, even more changes. The lawyer becomes a chef, then a kitchen designer; then he retires and goes into politics. The housewife becomes an image consultant, then an artist, business owner, and teacher. At every turn in your career path, you are summoned back into the deep waters within to explore the unfolding of your destiny. You may find yourself questioning the profession you once loved, or discovering that you want to follow an entirely different career path. This can be a difficult experience that includes making choices that others disagree with. Your courage is crucial. You need to be ready, willing, and able to listen to your inner voice, and follow it. Joseph Campbell called it "following your bliss." You know best who you are and what you're supposed to be doing, so go for it!

When you find yourself in a quandary about what career path to follow, consider taking time off from your daily schedule. Go on a vision quest, retreat, or camping trip, even if it's only for a few days. Once you're away from it all, jump into receiving your next set of life instructions. Watch your dreams; keep a journal; define your purpose in life; and make drawings, collages, or lists on what you love to do. Give voice to parts of yourself that aren't directly linked to producing an income. Stir the pot. Maintain your courage and trust yourself. Affirm: *"I am completely open to fulfilling my destiny. I call my next set of life instructions to myself now. My work in the world becomes more fulfilling, inspiring, and lucrative every day."*

### *Enhance the Career area of your home when:*

- you are seeking your purpose in life.
- you want to make a change in your current job or career.
- you want to volunteer or do meaningful community service work.
- you're moving from one vocation to another.
- you want to be more courageous.

### *Outer enhancements related to Career:*

- Water features such as fountains, waterfalls, and aquariums

- Artwork or photos depicting bodies of water, such as pools, streams, lakes, or the ocean
- Any image or object that personally symbolizes your career, such as books on your subject of expertise, or items with your company name
- Items that are free-form, flowing, or asymmetrically shaped
- Mirrors, crystals, and glass items
- Items in black or very dark tones
- Quotes, sayings, and affirmations related to courage and following one's path in life

## Inner Work Related to Knowledge and Self-Cultivation

Key Word: *Stillness*

The *I Ching's* trigram *Ken,* meaning "Still Mountain," is associated with knowledge and self-cultivation. You assimilate knowledge best, whether in school or in life, when you regularly allow your body and mind to be still. The mountain symbolizes climbing to a peaceful inner space where you can assimilate and integrate your daily experiences. Stillness, the Yin counterpart to Yang action, transforms your knowledge and adventures into wisdom. To be wise, you need quiet time to balance your active time. When you build quietude into your daily routine, you honor the full rhythm of life. This teaching reminds us all-too-busy Westerners that to be truly brilliant, creative, and productive, we must also embrace stillness.

Give yourself a daily gift of stillness. If you are not already practicing some form of meditation, introspection, or contemplation, begin now. There are literally hundreds of books and classes on how to quiet the mind and body. Some people find that it's easier to be still after some physical activity, such as dancing or exercising. If you are a beginner, start with five minutes a day, twice a day. You can begin now by sitting comfortably and watching your breath for a few moments. Focus on your inhalation and exhalation, and simply sit and breathe, refocusing on your breath whenever your attention wanders. By taking a time-out from being active every waking moment, you deepen the peace and wisdom residing within you. Affirm: *"I am wise and calm. Stillness enhances my peace and wisdom."*

***Enhance the Knowledge and Self-Cultivation area of your home when:***

- you are a student of any subject at any time.
- you are in counseling or engaged in any self-growth activity.
- you want to cultivate wisdom and peace of mind.

***Outer enhancements related to Knowledge and Self-Cultivation:***

- Books, tapes, or other material that you are currently studying
- Art that portrays mountains or quiet places, such as meditation gardens
- Pictures or photographs of people you consider accomplished and wise
- Items in the colors of black, blue, or green
- Meditative and inspirational sayings, quotes, or affirmations

## Inner Work Related to the Center

The Center of the Bagua Map is considered the hub of the wheel, or the "solar plexus" of the house. The element of Earth finds a home here, symbolizing the importance of arranging our lives to flow around a solid, grounded base. Many traditional Chinese homes had a central earthen courtyard where earth Ch'i was directly available to the inhabitants. If there is space in the Center of your home, that would be an excellent location for a courtyard, atrium, or potted plants. Otherwise, you can display art that reminds you to stay centered and connected with the earth. Because of its association with the earth, ceramics and yellow and earth-tone colors can also enhance the Center of your home.

Determine how grounded and connected to your Center you feel at this time. Nurture your ability to remain centered through life's many changes by directly connecting with the earth every day. Take a walk, sit on the earth, or literally put your hands in the soil by planting or mulching a garden. Watch how your inner being becomes stronger and more centered as you connect with the earth. Say affirmations such as: *"I remain grounded and centered all the time. I am always in the secure and loving embrace of Mother Earth."*

## BAGUA MAP EXERCISE

COLLECT IMAGES THAT DEPICT THE BAGUA AREA YOU'RE WORK-ING WITH, LIKE THOSE OF YOUR IDEAL PARTNER, JOB, FAMILY, HEALTH OR FINANCIAL SITUATION, AND MAKE THEM INTO A COLLAGE. WHEN YOU EXPRESS YOURSELF ARTISTICALLY, YOU ARE LITERALLY GATHERING CH'I TO ENHANCE YOUR LIFE. YOU CAN DRAW, PAINT, WEAVE, BUILD, OR SCULPT IMAGES THAT SYMBOLIZE YOUR GOALS. ASK YOURSELF QUESTIONS SUCH AS: WHAT COLOR IS MY HEALTH? WHAT SHAPE IS MY REPUTATION? WHAT IMAGE IS MY CAREER? SURPRISINGLY POW-ERFUL ANSWERS OFTEN COME FROM THIS PROCESS. YOUR OWN ART STRIKES A VERY PERSONAL CHORD AS THE TANGIBLE EXPRESSION OF YOUR INNER QUEST. BE SURE TO DISPLAY IT, IF ONLY TEMPORARILY, SO THAT YOUR CHOSEN IMAGES CAN NURTURE AND SUSTAIN YOUR GOALS.

# Chapter Three

# YIN AND YANG
# AND THE FIVE ELEMENTS—
# NATURE'S ABUNDANT PALETTE

*"Every time we create a straight line, we need a curve for balance . . . the curve of a vase, the sinuous line of a chair, the sweep of an oval table, the plump upholstery of a sofa. These things take the edges of modernity, making it sensuous and appealing."*

— Ilse Crawford

## *Yin and Yang*

We are the "Goldilocks species," meaning that we like our environments to be not too cold or hot, not too dark or light, not too small or large, but juuussst right. We like a balance between the two extremes called Yin and Yang. On one extreme, Yin is associated with curved shapes and small, cold, dark, wet, or ornate settings and items. On the other extreme, Yang is associated with angular shapes and large, light, hot, or open settings and items. Feng Shui observes that the more extreme our home designs are, the more uncomfortable they may feel to us. Most people are happiest and most comfortable with a balanced mix of Yin and Yang features in their environments.

Western architecture and design is often quite Yang, with a plethora of angles, high ceilings, big pieces of furniture, huge windows, and sharp corners. In the midst of this, it's easy to see why Feng Shui practitioners often suggest softer, rounder, more Yin shapes and furnishings to balance those Yang environments. We may love high ceilings, huge white expanses, and bright lights in our art galleries, churches, and shopping malls, but at some point, we're ready to return to the cozy, comfortable place we call home, where everything's just right.

Although our culture tends to lean toward Yang architecture, the Yin extreme can also be found. Picture a room that is small and cavelike; with dark furniture, dim lighting, and a low ceiling. Many basements are like this. Yang components, such as additional lighting; large mirrors; and warm, light colors are needed to balance the many Yin features. Much more common is the room that is large and angular, with a high ceiling, white walls, big windows, sizable art pieces, and light-colored furniture. Here, Yin components such as rounded tables; ornate window treatments; rugs; and dark, rich colors are needed to create balance and comfort.

Each room in your home needs to be approached individually. A bedroom can be quite Yin—soft duvets, ornate patterns, fluffy pillows, low lighting—and still be comfortable because its function as a place to rest and rejuvenate is primarily Yin. Even so, there's always a balance. Too many pillows, too many little bottles on the bureau, and too many layers of lace and fabric can tilt the balance. On the other hand, a home office, with its Yang components—such as a large desk, bright lights, and business equipment, can be just what you need to get the job done. However, too many sharp angles and hard surfaces can leave you feeling irritated and stressed out. When Yin and Yang are balanced, you experience each room in your home as comfortable and beautiful—a personal paradise that nourishes and protects your health, happiness, and prosperity.

Take a moment to look at the room that you're sitting in now. Using the chart that follows, make a list of the Yin and Yang features, and determine if either dominates. Decide if there are things that you would add or subtract to the room to heighten its Yin/Yang balance.

```
┌─────────────────────────────────────────────────────────┐
│                    YIN/YANG CHART                         │
│                                                           │
│   Yin          Yang      │    Yin          Yang           │
│                          │                                │
│   Dark         Light     │    Low          High           │
│   Small        Large     │    Cool         Warm           │
│   Ornate       Plain     │    Cold         Hot            │
│   Horizontal   Vertical  │    Floral       Geometric      │
│   Curved       Straight  │    Earth        Sky            │
│   Rounded      Angular   │    Moon         Sun            │
│   Soft         Hard      │    Feminine     Masculine      │
└─────────────────────────────────────────────────────────┘
```

### The Five Elements

In Feng Shui, the elements Wood, Fire, Earth, Metal, and Water are considered the basic building blocks of everything physical on the planet. They manifest in countless ways and combinations all around us. Feng Shui observes that human beings are made up of all Five Elements, and therefore, we are most comfortable when they're all present in our homes. The fastest way to learn how to work with the elements is to observe them in your home.

Although many people can sense when an environment is out of balance, they often don't know exactly how to fix it. Would red or blue be good here? Should the table be round or rectangular? Is a mirror or artwork best there? Questions such as these are easily answered when you know how to read the elements, making them one of your most intriguing Feng Shui tools. Learn how to recognize and combine the Five Elements, and you'll be able to see exactly what each room needs to bring it into perfect balance.

### An Overall Elemental Reading

To determine the overall elemental balance of a room, use the following lists of associations related to the Five Elements. Note the things made out of the elements themselves, such as wooden or metal furnishings. Find those items that are associated with an element such as a marble tabletop (Metal), a mirror (Water), or plants (Wood). Look for colors associated with each element, such as red (Fire), blues and greens (Wood), or yellow (Earth). Note that the darker a color gets, the more "Watery" it becomes, such as black, navy blue, and dark brown; while the lighter a color gets, the more it becomes associated with Metal. Look at your artwork to see what element it portrays, such as a "Fiery" sunset painting or a "Watery" oceanscape. Take an overall reading, and note whether there are elements that dominate, are barely represented, or are missing entirely from the room.

One of my clients lives in a beautiful home near the ocean. As I looked at her living room, I could see that all the elements except Earth were perfectly represented. Unlike most rooms, there were no square furnishings or decorations. Except for a book, and picture frames here and there, everything was soft and rounded, with no yellow or earthtones in sight. I asked her if she had a piece of yellow cloth. She produced a golden yellow T-shirt and we draped it around a sofa pillow. The effect was stunning. The whole room suddenly had a center, a place from which everything else pivoted and flowed. All the room needed was one simple addition to bring it into perfect balance.

### The Wood Element

Energetically, the Wood element fosters your intuition, creativity, flexibility, and expansion. When there's too much Wood in an environment, it can promote a sense of being overwhelmed or overcommitted, while too little Wood can stagnate growth and impede intuitive and creative flow.

*The Wood element is found in:*

- wooden furniture, paneling, and accessories.
- all plants and flowers, including silk, plastic, and dried plants.
- plant-based cloth and textiles, such as cotton and rayon.
- floral upholstery, wall coverings, draperies, and linens.
- art portraying landscapes, gardens, plants, and flowers.
- columnar shapes, such as pillars, pedestals, and poles.
- paper.

- stripes.
- blue and green tones.

### The Fire Element

The Fire element activates leadership qualities and kindles healthy emotional interactions between people. Too much Fire in an environment stimulates or amplifies aggression, impatience, and impulsive behavior, while too little Fire can promote emotional darkness or coldness.

*The Fire element is found in:*

- lighting, including electric, oil, candles, fireplaces, and natural sunlight.
- items from animals, such as fur, suede, leather, bone, feathers, silk, and wool
- pets and wildlife.
- art portraying people or animals.
- art depicting sunshine, fire, or other illumination.
- triangles, pyramids, and cone shapes.
- all red tones, including pink, red-orange, magenta, and maroon.

### The Earth Element

The Earth element enhances physical strength, sensuality, order, practicality, and stability. Too much Earth in a home creates an atmosphere that is heavy, serious, or conservative, while too little of the Earth element promotes instability, clutter, and chaos.

*The Earth element is found in:*

- adobe, brick, and tile.
- ceramics and earthenware objects.
- square and rectangular shapes.
- art portraying earthy landscapes, such as deserts or fertile fields.
- yellow and all earthtones.

### *The Metal Element*

The Metal element enhances mental acuity and independence, and strengthens presence of mind, even in times of stress. Too much Metal creates mental rigidity, stubbornness, lack of teamwork, and the inability to compromise; while too little Metal promotes indecisiveness, procrastination, and confusion.

*The Metal element is found in:*

- all metals, including stainless steel, copper, brass, iron, silver, aluminum, and gold.
- cement, rocks, and stones—including marble, granite, and flagstone.
- natural crystals and gemstones.
- art and sculpture made from metal or stone.
- circular, oval, and arched shapes.
- white and light pastel colors.

### *The Water Element*

The Water element enhances spirituality, inspiration, relaxation, and the ability to go with the flow. Too much Water in an environment can promote spaciness and diminish productivity, while too little Water encourages stress, rivalry, anxiety, pettiness, and sarcasm.

*The Water element is found in:*

- streams, pools, fountains, and water features of all kinds.
- reflective surfaces such as cut crystal, glass, and mirrors.
- flowing, free-form, and asymmetrical shapes.
- art portraying bodies of water.
- black and all dark tones, such as charcoal gray and navy blue.

### *Artful Elemental Combinations*

As you are learning to identify the Five Elements, you'll notice that there are many things that combine several, or all of them. An aquarium, traditionally favored in Feng Shui for its Ch'i-enhancing qualities, gathers all the elements together in one pleasing combination, as shown in Figure 3A.

**FIGURE 3A**
*Aquariums bring the Five Elements together in one harmonious display. The water and glass container represent the Water element; the plants express Wood; the fish symbolize Fire; the sand represents Earth; and the rocks symbolize the Metal element.*

Aquariums are one of countless ways in which you can harmoniously bring all the elements together. Figures 3B and 3C show examples of how you can create Five Element groupings in your home by working with your own favorite colors, cherishables, and furnishings. As you can see, the Five Elements can really help you decide what colors and shapes to choose when creating beautiful arrangements anywhere in your home.

**FIGURE 3B**

*This inviting foyer arrangement includes all the elements. The flower arrangement represents Wood; the large red flowers and small birds add Fire; the rectangular shape and detailing of the mirror bring in Earth; the half-circular table and white bowl capture Metal; and the mirror, representing water, completes the elemental arrangement.*
***(Also in color, page 114.)***

**FIGURE 3C**

*A glass and metal coffee table, elementally representing Water and Metal, is complemented by a burgundy red candle (Fire), square books (Earth), and flowers (Wood). This arrangement brings the Five Elements together in one harmonious design.*

Five Element arrangements can be made in any room and can be any size that's appropriate for the space. I often suggest that people put together an elemental arrangement of objects in areas that need energizing, such as a garage, spare bedroom, or basement. This positive action marks the beginning of change and stimulates the Ch'i so that it's easier for people to organize these areas.

**FIGURE 3D**

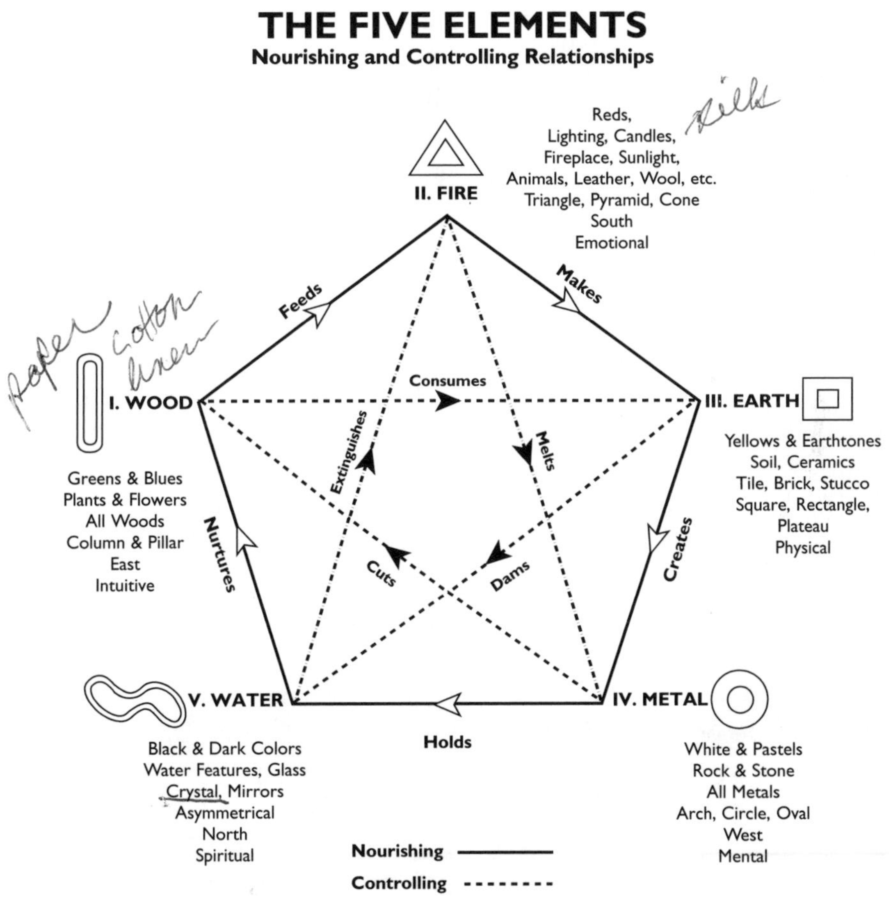

# THE FIVE ELEMENTS
**Nourishing and Controlling Relationships**

**II. FIRE**
Reds,
Lighting, Candles,
Fireplace, Sunlight,
Animals, Leather, Wool, etc.
Triangle, Pyramid, Cone
South
Emotional

**I. WOOD**
Greens & Blues
Plants & Flowers
All Woods
Column & Pillar
East
Intuitive

**III. EARTH**
Yellows & Earthtones
Soil, Ceramics
Tile, Brick, Stucco
Square, Rectangle,
Plateau
Physical

**V. WATER**
Black & Dark Colors
Water Features, Glass
Crystal, Mirrors
Asymmetrical
North
Spiritual

**IV. METAL**
White & Pastels
Rock & Stone
All Metals
Arch, Circle, Oval
West
Mental

Feeds — Makes — Consumes — Melts — Extinguishes — Cuts — Dams — Creates — Nurtures — Holds

Nourishing ———
Controlling - - - - - - -

### *The Nourishing Cycle of the Five Elements*

When you bring the Five Elements into a room, you are tapping into their Nourishing Cycle, where each element feeds and sustains the other in perfect harmony. Water sustains Wood; Wood feeds Fire; Fire makes Earth; Earth creates Metal; and Metal holds Water. The Nourishing Cycle shows us how the elements strengthen and nurture each other in an endless regenerating sequence. When all five are present in an environment, a natural balance is achieved.

### *The Controlling Cycle of the Five Elements*

In the Controlling Cycle, we see how the elements dominate and control each other. In this cycle, Wood consumes Earth; Earth dams Water; Water extinguishes Fire; Fire melts Metal; and Metal cuts Wood. The Controlling Cycle is regarded as a powerful guide for establishing elemental harmony, and is present in many of the places we consider the most beautiful. A palm tree oasis in the desert is a perfect example of Wood consuming Earth, while a tropical island in crystal-clear water is essentially Earth damming Water. Nature constantly provides us with examples of how the Controlling Cycle of the elements can create harmony and beauty.

It's also very useful to be aware of the Controlling Cycle when you're balancing the elements in your home. When one element is especially dominant, the Controlling Cycle will show you the element that can quickly balance the Ch'i. Once you have balanced the dominant element with its controlling partner, you can turn to the Nourishing Cycle and further refine your elemental work.

I worked with a home where the living room was dominated by Earth. The decor included square tile floors, stucco walls, dark beige-checked couches, brown chairs, small square area rugs in various earth-tones, and many small earthenware accessories. The furniture was arranged in a tight square around a large rectangular table made up of ceramic tiles. On the wall behind the sofa hung a painting of the desert. So much Earth gave the space a heavy, boxed-in feeling, which matched the way the owners felt in the room.

To balance the Earth, they needed to first introduce the element that controlled Earth, which is Wood. They added turquoise pillows to the sofa, a large textured rug in blues and greens beneath the coffee table, and several large plants. Turning to the Nourishing Cycle, they fed the Wood element with Water by replacing their desert painting with a large mirror and adding a small tabletop waterfall. They also introduced the Metal element by framing that mirror in a gilt frame and arranging the plants in round metal pots. Lamplight, natural light, and touches of coral painted on their ceramics brought in plenty of Fire, which by nature strengthens Earth.

They also opened up the boxy "Earthy" furniture arrangement by turning the two brown chairs at a diagonal, giving them a peripheral view of the door. As a finishing touch, they ran a turquoise table runner diagonally across the coffee table to soften two of the corners. With these changes, their once-constricted living room became very comfortable, inviting a more spontaneous and enjoyable lifestyle.

Elemental extremes abound in our architecture and rooms. Monochromatic motifs, and the constant repeating of one shape, are two things I often see in people's homes. Although the effect may be perceived as quite trendy or dramatic, most people will not find comfort there, because on the elemental level, one is dominating while others are missing. Remember, your ultimate goal is to bring all Five Elements into balance in every room. It's remarkable to witness the difference this makes in the perceived comfort of a room.

### A QUICK REFERENCE FOR WORKING WITH THE CONTROLLING CYCLE

When the dominating element is Wood:
Bring in the Controlling element of Metal,
Highlight with Earth and Fire,
Refine as needed with touches of Water.

When the dominant element is Fire:
Bring in the Controlling element of Water,
Highlight with Metal and Earth,
Refine as needed with touches of Wood.

When the dominant element is Earth:
Bring in the Controlling element of Wood,
Highlight with Water and Metal,
Refine as needed with touches of Fire.

When the dominant element is Metal:
Bring in the Controlling element of Fire,
Highlight with Wood and Water,
Refine as needed with touches of Earth.

When the dominant element is Water:
Bring in the Controlling element of Earth,
Highlight with Fire and Wood,
Refine as needed with touches of Metal.

### *Elemental Fluency*

Practice identifying the Five Elements, and study their interplay in your home, your friends' homes, restaurants, stores, and in your workplace. As you do, you are learning an important part of Feng Shui alchemy. There is a magical moment when you realize that you have become fluent in a language that benefits you and everyone around you. And from that point forward, you'll be able to create environments that are balanced and vibrant in every way.

# *Chapter Four*

# CH'I ENHANCEMENTS—
# ROMANCING THE HOME

*"In the end, all that really matters is that we approach*
*wherever we live with full attention and an open heart . . .*
*a bouquet of flowers, a song, the smell of freshly baked*
*bread, an affectionate embrace, such things can trans-*
*form any place into a happy, heartwarming abode."*
— Thomas Bender

Feng Shui focuses on enhancing the harmony and vitality of your environment. Surrounding yourself with things that lift your spirits and deepen your love for life is a primary goal. So romance your home—and yourself—by living with things that enhance the Ch'i.

Surround yourself with only those items that pass the "I love this!" test. Some people like to fill a room with big plants and bright fabrics, while others prefer a single floral arrangement and muted colors. One couple actually chose a large model of the USS Enterprise to enhance their Wealth and Prosperity area, since *Star Trek* made them feel rich and powerful. This was a creative choice that I would never have imagined, but it worked for them!

Ch'i is always enhanced by your joy, inspiration, and creativity. Feng Shui invites you to pour your individuality into your home—room by room—in exactly the way you find most appealing.

## *Art*

The colors and images in your art reflect aspects of yourself that can build you up or tear you down. Ideally, your artwork elicits positive feelings and acts as an environmental affirmation throughout your home. Art depicting violent, emotionally upsetting, contorted, or dead subject matter is not recommended.

I often see a certain phenomenon I call Therapy Art. This is art that reflects a person's inner journey at a particular time, often long since past. In one case, I worked with a woman who had collected several pen-and-ink drawings by one artist. Each drawing was of a naked woman in a compromised position. In one of the pieces, the woman was being auctioned off from a slave block. In another, she was the only naked person in a large crowd. When I asked my client how she felt about her art, she said she had collected it while she was in therapy ten years ago. They had symbolized her healing journey, one she was now completing. She realized that the drawings kept her visually anchored to her past pain, and that it was time to let them go. When she did, she noticed that her whole self-image improved.

**FIGURE 4A**
*Art can be chosen to enhance specific Bagua areas in the home. This painting of vibrant flowers by Monte deGraw strengthens health and vitality in the Health and Family area located in the living room.*
**(Also in color, page 114.)**

**FIGURE 4B**

*When the Health and Family area is in the bedroom, the art you choose may be different. Jeff Kahn's painting of two vibrantly healthy people is more intimate and fits well into a bedroom.* **(Also in color, page 115.)**

Therapy Art is not necessarily bad, but like medicine, it serves its purpose and then is no longer needed. To continue to take it is unnecessary and often detrimental. Give yourself permission to let go of any art that you don't like, or that drags you back to a place you'd rather leave behind. Your art should be an accurate reflection of your inspired self—a window into an uplifting, heavenly experience.

Frequently, clients have art that they've never liked, but because it's something that's been in the family for years, they feel obliged to live with it. There's a prime example of this in my own family. My mother has a large portrait of a great-aunt hanging over the mantel in the living room. The aunt's expression is stern, and her eyes appear to stare at people no matter where they sit. Throughout my childhood, we never used that room, and I believe it's because of the unsettling portrait. When I asked my mother if she liked this painting, her answer was an immediate no, but she had tolerated it over the years because it was an heirloom. Generations had suffered under my old aunt's glower. My mother added that she was planning on giving it to me! I told her I'd be happy to donate it to a historic home, where visitors could enjoy those eyes for a brief moment or two, then move on. If you have an heirloom you don't like or want, it's time to let it go—to a family member who does want it, an antique dealer, or a charity. Reminders of the past are only good when they take you to a place you want to go.

Your art can also be matched with the function of the room and the Bagua Map, to create a dynamic Ch'i enhancement. This kind of "layering" doubly encourages and supports specific aspects of your life. For instance, when your Health and Family area is in your living room, choose art that represents health and vitality to you, and is also appropriate for your living room area (Figure 4A). If your Health and Family area happens to fall in your bedroom, you may pick an entirely different piece, as in Figure 4B.

**FIGURE 4C**

*Here, art from Tibet is displayed in the Career area of a living room, beautifying the space and reminding owners to remain purposeful in their work.*

Spiritual art that is meaningful to you is also a potent way to attract and uplift Ch'i. This includes images of angels, saints, great teachers, gods, goddesses, and mystics. The hand-painted Tibetan mandala and the statue in Figure 4C are located in the Career area of a couple's living room, reminding them to remain purposeful in their work. Here again, the key is to choose symbols that have personal, inspirational meaning for you. Place spiritual art in any Bagua area where you seek improvement.

Original art, like the kind you see in Figures 4A, 4B, and 4C, carries tremendous Ch'i. Your creativity and artistry should be an integral part of your home. Whether it's watercolors, photographs, ceramics, weavings, or collages, any art that you or your family have made and are proud of is powerful. Surround yourself with it, and feel the energy that flows through your home as a result. Original art, touched directly by the artist's hand, also carries a concentrated amount of Ch'i. When you buy local artists' works, you are benefitting from their creativity while supporting your community. Although only a few of us can afford the original art of the great masters, most of us *can* afford the creative works of our local artists.

Take a few moments to look *into* the art you have collected. What part of you does each piece represent? Do you like what you see? If not, make it a priority to let it go and replace it with art that you really love. Your art, like everything else that surrounds you, is meant to lift and nurture you on a daily basis. Enjoy collecting art that reflects your goals and dreams. Express yourself, and relish the process of creating a home that is, in itself, an "original."

### Color

Color can be a tremendous Ch'i enhancement when you love it, or cause a real depletion in energy if you don't. If a color bugs you, get rid of it. It could save your marriage or your sanity or both, as one couple recently discovered. Two weeks after they'd moved into their "new" fixer-upper home, they were fighting like they never had before. One look at the wallpaper in their large kitchen and family room told me why. The former owners must have bought the entire stock of pea green and old gold wallpaper, and covered a 20-by-20-foot-square area with it. The couple had planned to take the paper down eventually, but after their fights (and our consultation), they started peeling it off immediately. Removing the offensive colors made a positive change in the entire house—and in their moods!

Color is powerful and personal. The colors that one person likes, another person can't stand. And like all Ch'i enhancements, color is optional. Use the colors associated with the Five Elements and the Bagua Map only if you love them. If not, choose another way to enhance the space. Keep in mind that each basic color includes a wide spectrum of tones and hues. Red, associated with the Fire element; and the Wealth and Prosperity, Fame and Reputation, and Love and Marriage Bagua areas, is present in all red tones, from light pink to Chinese red to dark burgundy. Your color choices may be subtle, bright, vivid, dark, or subdued. It's completely up to you. Stay within the palette you are attracted to, and your color choices will create an atmosphere you'll enjoy every day.

Color can be introduced in a number of ways. Blues and greens, associated with the Wood element, and with the Knowledge and Self-Cultivation, and Health and Family Bagua areas, can be brought in with vases, books, and furniture. Or, walls can be painted in attractive shades of green, teal, or blue. A client whose Health and Family area is in her garage arranged a collection of items that she enjoys every time she gets in or out of her car. It consists of a poster of an herb garden, dark green silk ivy in a turquoise glass vase, and several bright blue and green bottles containing fragrant oils. Although she was already in good health when she made this arrangement, she noticed that she has even more energy and vitality than before.

Color can nurture your soul as food nourishes your body. Determine what colors are your favorites. Which ones feed you right down to your bones, and energize and heal you? Whatever colors they are, make sure that you have them somewhere in your environment. Choose items in your colors, such as fabrics, vases, dishes, and flowers, and place them where they can feed you with a glance. Whether it's the violet light within an amethyst crystal or the vibrant turquoise glaze on a favorite mug, feast on the colors that nourish you.

(Color is also discussed in Chapter 6 on Living Rooms.)

### *Crystals*

Round, faceted cut-glass crystals, as shown in Figure 4D, modulate the Ch'i flow around extreme architectural features. Compact in size, they are often used where there is no room for any other kind of enhancement. For instance, crystals can be hung from the ceiling near a sharp angle or corner that protrudes invasively into a room, reducing the sharpness of the corner while balancing Ch'i circulation.

**FIGURE 4D**

*Cut-glass crystals modulate Ch'i flow and are used in halls, windows, and architectural challenges such as sharp corners, angles, hallways, and stairways.*

Traditionally, crystals are hung on nine-inch lengths (or multiples of nine) of red string. Here in the West, length and color of string are often chosen to match the application. Some people do not want to advertise their crystals by using red string, so they choose clear filament instead. Others want to hang a crystal just an inch or two from the ceiling to keep it out of harm's way. Use your judgment, knowing that the crystal will do its job in any case. They range in size from 10 to 75 millimeters (mm), with 25 or 30mm being the most popular sizes for Feng Shui purposes.

**FIGURE 4E**

*A round-faceted crystal suspended from the center of the ceiling lifts and circulates the Ch'i in this small bathroom.*

In bathrooms, crystals counteract the draining effects of sink, toilet, and bath plumbing by lifting and circulating the Ch'i. Hang one crystal from the ceiling midway between toilet and door, or in the middle of the room when the toilet can be seen from the bathroom door, as in Figure 4E.

Crystals can also modulate the raging Ch'i in long hallways. Hang them well above head level about ten feet apart, or use one or more faceted crystal light fixtures to achieve the same effect. To temper the waterfall of Ch'i that sweeps down a long stairway, hang a crystal, or crystal light fixture, over the bottom stair.

Windows with views that pull you across the room have the same effect on Ch'i. To help catch and circulate the Ch'i, hang a crystal in front of any large window (Figure 4D), especially one with a grand view. To balance the Ch'i flow between two doors, or a door and window located directly across from each other, hang a crystal midway between them.

(**Please note:** *Crystals hung in windows that receive bright sunlight have caused fires. If your window is exposed to direct hot sun, either hang the crystal at a safe distance and height, or choose another enhancement.*)

When a room seems stagnant or in need of cleansing, suspend a crystal in the center of the room. This works best when it is the only crystal in the room, as it circulates one clear, clean ripple of Ch'i throughout. Guard against using too many crystals in one room or area. Too many ripples coming from multiple crystals can interfere with, rather than enhance, balanced Ch'i flow.

Your crystals symbolize the healthy, happy circulation of Ch'i through your body, mind, and spirit. They represent your ability to pace yourself. If you experience life as going too fast or too slow, you need to modulate the flow. Take some time to become crystal clear about the lifestyle changes you can make that'll make your pace just right.

### Lighting

Lighting is an easy way to enhance the Ch'i in your home. This includes incandescent and halogen electric lights, as well as candles, oil lamps, fireplaces, and natural sunlight. Lighting can fill a dark corner (as in Figure 4F), lift a low ceiling, camouflage a sharp angle, or brighten up a gloomy room. Because we are always seeking balance, we don't want to over-light or under-light any area. Put your lighting on dimmer switches so that you can create the mood you want at any particular moment, and put some of your lights on timers so that you never come home to a dark house. When building your home, give serious thought to your lighting needs, and install wall sconces, as well as recessed, accent, display, and track lighting and outlets. As with other basic Ch'i enhancements, lighting can be chosen to represent the colors or element associated with a Bagua area, such as the table lamp in Figure 4G. When using a light to energize a Bagua area, consider leaving it on most or all the time until you experience a positive change.

**FIGURE 4F**

*Attractive lighting enhances Ch'i and is often used in Feng Shui to soften and brighten corners.*

**FIGURE 4G**

*This artful lamp, with its harbor theme, has been purposely located in the Helpful People and Travel area of the house.*

In its ideal state, your lighting is art. Choose light fixtures and lamps that add character to your decor. Arrange your lamps with other cherished items, and let the light that fills your home reflect the creativity and light within you. If there is a dark area in your home, notice what part of the Bagua Map it correlates with. Often, the dark areas in your home correspond with darkened areas in your life. Refer to the Bagua Map (Chapter 2) for specific guidance on how to "en-light-en" your inner world while bringing beautiful lighting into your home environment.

**Fluorescent Lights:** Although they are energy efficient, standard and "stick-up" fluorescent lights buzz audibly, flicker, and emit only part of the light spectrum. They are famous for casting an unnatural, sickly glare over everything and everyone, and they can deplete Ch'i, especially when located directly overhead. Full-spectrum fluorescent bulbs help, but the buzzing and flickering remain, so they are not recommended in places where you spend much time, such as kitchens and offices. Rely instead on the warmth of incandescent or halogen lighting. I have visited many kitchens where the overhead fluorescent lights were identified as a primary source of irritation in the family's life. When replaced with warmer lighting, the kitchen became a comfortable, attractive place to spend time preparing home-cooked meals with friends and family. In the home and office, remove the fluorescent bulbs located directly overhead, and install task lighting nearby. You'll be amazed at the improvement in your energy level..

**Night-lights:** Eliminate the hazards of groping around in the dark by using night-lights. They come in a variety of attractive shapes and colors, and can be the difference between danger and safety in hallways, stairways, bathrooms, attics, basements, closets, and other dark places.

**Fireplaces and Candles:** Fireplaces can be a wonderful source of heat and light and are powerful representations of the Fire element. Yet, because they are often large features, they can be too fiery and actually burn up the Ch'i in a room. You can elementally balance a fireplace by adding a symbol of the Water element nearby, such as a water feature, mirror, glass fireplace doors, or any kind of crystal ornamentation. Keep the fireplace clean and arranged with fresh logs for your next fire. Place healthy plants, fresh flowers, or any kind of artful screening in front of the fireplace opening when not in use.

**FIGURE 4H**

*Before Feng Shui enhancements, the fiery art above the fireplace, the surrounding dried plant material, and the charred logs suggested a parched environment in perpetual danger of going up in flames.*

**FIGURE 4I**

*The balancing influences of the mirror, decorative screen, living plants, and meaningful nature objects cool and balance the fireplace area. Other Feng Shui improvements include the relocation of the television into a closed cabinet (seen in the mirror's reflection), and the rearrangement of furniture to encourage conversation and family interaction.*

Figures 4H and 4I show one example of how a fireplace can be balanced. Figure 4H shows fiery art displayed over an unkempt fireplace. Old, dried plant material around the hearth suggests tinder ready to go up in flames, promoting irritability and a sense of danger. The family had many heated disagreements and emotional outbursts here, symptoms of an overabundance of the Fire element. Figure 4I shows a more balanced living environment, with the fiery art and surrounding tinder replaced by a mirror, fan screen, and living plants. Pine cones gathered during a relaxing vacation were kept to remind family members to relax and enjoy life. These simple changes balanced the Ch'i, bringing the invaluable gift of peace and harmony to the household.

When not in use, fireplaces can become grottos where beautiful arrangements of nature objects, statuary, or candles can be displayed, as in Figure 4J.

**FIGURE 4J**

*During the summer months, this fireplace becomes a "candleplace." Sand covers the floor of the fireplace, supporting various arrangements of candles and holders throughout the warm season.* **(Also in color, page 115.)**

Candles, another type of lighting that enhances Ch'i, bring light and warmth into a room, and provide an easy way to experiment with new colors and shapes. They can be used to energize a Bagua area or symbolize one or more of the Five Elements. Candles are also wonderful mood makers, whether it's an introspective mood in the sanctuary, an intimate mood in the bedroom, or an atmosphere of warmth and good cheer in living and dining rooms. The best candles are dripless, and either unscented or naturally scented.

### Living Things

Living things, including healthy plants, flowers, pets, and wildlife, are carriers of vital energy. They bring the allure of nature indoors, add life and color to our homes, and enhance our appreciation for life.

**Plants:** Plants are superb Ch'i enhancements when they are healthy and vibrant. They provide a sampling of nature's variety and beauty, and help us to stay connected with the wonder of the natural world. They also provide us with the fundamental benefit of cleaning the air around us. Choose plants with a friendly appearance, such as those with wide, rounded leaves or a generally soft, graceful appearance. There are many varieties of plants in this category, including schefflera, philodendron, pothos, jade, croton, ivy, Chinese evergreen, peace lily, fichus, and most dracenas and palms.

Plants with an unfriendly sharp or spiky appearance are not recommended unless they are far removed from people. These include dracena marginata, sago palm, yucca, and most cacti and bromeliads. If you have plants like this and want to keep them, group them safely away from people with other friendlier plants.

When clients who had a home business invited me over, I was greeted by spiky cacti growing in pots along their front walkway. The abundant thorns did not communicate my clients' desire to expand their customer base and their business opportunities. They moved their cactus collection away from the pathway where it could be enjoyed from a distance, and highlighted the walkway with pots of flowers and herbs. Business immediately improved. The friendly new plants, symbols of welcome, paved the way for customers and opportunities to flow through their door.

Plants are often used in Feng Shui to soften the sharp angles and corners found in furnishings and architecture. Vining plants such as pothos and ivy can camouflage sharp corners on furniture, while lush floor plants are excellent for filling in corners or softening angles that project into a room. One well-chosen plant can transform a room, as we often see in design magazines. When choosing the right plant for your needs, make sure to match the plant's growth habit and light requirements with the location. Many varieties of indoor plants that have been developed to thrive in low light conditions are slow growers, such as most dracenas, aglonemas, and ferns. On the other hand, many indoor plants that bloom need very bright light to be happy. When necessary, install additional lighting to assure their health and vitality.

When a plant becomes diseased or unsightly, it is best to replace it. Don't spend too long trying to nurse a plant back to health unless you have a greenhouse or area specifically set up as a plant hospital. Healthy, vibrant plants improve the Ch'i; unhealthy ones do not. Consider hiring a plant service to provide ongoing plant maintenance and to replace plants when necessary.

Be sure to install your plants in planters or containers that are pleasing to the eye and the spirit. Rely on the Five Elements and the Bagua Map to help you choose containers in colors, shapes, and materials that correspond to the area or element you are working with. Make sure to protect your floors and furniture from spills or condensation with waterproof saucers or mats.

Silk plants can be used in areas that are too dark, too high, or unattended for long periods of time. As long as they look healthy and alive, they are viable substitutes for living plant material. Bend and shape branches and leaves to give them a more natural appearance. Silk plants tend to last longer than silk flowers, approximately 18 to 24 months. Dust them with a hair dryer, and clean them with silk plant cleaner on a regular basis. Because dried branches and plants often look dead, they are not recommended to enhance the Ch'i.

**Flowers:** Fresh flowers add color and sensuality to any room. "Flowers are nature's courtesans," says Ilse Crawford in *The Sensual*

*House.* "They elevate the mood, perfume the air, and can be edible and medicinal." A flower bouquet in multiple colors embodies the living dance of the Five Elements, while flowers in a single color can highlight an individual element. Red tulips, carnations, or roses will ignite the Fire element, while white mums or daisies strengthen the Metal element. Flowers can also be artfully chosen to enhance the Bagua areas in your home, such as two pink roses in your Love and Marriage area, or deep purple irises in your Career area.

(**Please note:** *Just as flowers can lift the Ch'i, they can drop the Ch'i if not properly cared for. Keep your flowers as long as they look vibrant and fresh. Once they begin to decline, groom or replace them immediately.)*

**FIGURE 4K**

*This is a perfect example of "dead" dried flowers, found next to the fireplace pictured in Figure 4G.*

**FIGURE 4L**

*These "fresh" dried flowers grace a guest cottage and are replaced seasonally.*

Dried flowers, including wreaths, swags, and arrangements, are an alternative to fresh flowers, but they have a life span that isn't as long as most people assume. Many Feng Shui practitioners advise against the use of dried flowers for this reason. Dried flowers lose their vibrancy—their Ch'i—after three to four months. And, as with fresh flowers, they can deplete an environment if kept past their prime. I've visited homes where the dried flowers had died years ago and were depleting rather than enhancing the Ch'i, as in Figure 4K. With this in mind, enjoy dried flowers such as the ones in Figure 4L, as you would a long-lasting fresh flower arrangement, not as a permanent decoration.

Potpourri is often frowned upon in Feng Shui for the same reason as dried flowers. People tend to keep it long after it has lost its Ch'i-enhancing qualities. If you love potpourri, choose a mix made from natural components, and be sure to replace it as soon as it loses its scent, which can be as often as once a week. Potpourri that's naturally scented with essential oils is best. You can also make your own by mixing newly dried petals, pods, and leaves with your favorite scented oils.

Silk and plastic flowers are alternatives to fresh and dried flowers. They have a longer life span than either fresh or dried flowers and will usually maintain their vibrancy for about a year. Be sure to clean them on a regular basis.

**FIGURE 4M**

*A living Ch'i enhancement at its finest—if you like cats. Garfield is loved and adored by his family, and he keeps the house lively with his antics.*

**Pets:** Pets, such as Garfield in Figure 4M, are natural batteries of Ch'i, and they can bring the loving spirit out in just about anyone. It is well known that bringing pets into hospitals and retirement homes strengthens the health and well-being of patients and residents alike. As is always the case in Feng Shui, the key is care. When you treat your pets with love and dignity, they bring tremendous energy into a home.

When your pets spend time indoors, make sure they have a special spot within your home. Dogs and cats need a bed, rug, or mat that is all theirs, while smaller animals need their own cages or tanks that give them plenty of room to grow and live happy, healthy lives. Keep pet homes fresh and clean to assure the health and vitality of your pets, as well as the quality of Ch'i flowing through your home. Please do not allow anyone—child or adult—to abuse or neglect a pet. It's not only cruel, but it depletes the energy in the entire home. Teach children to care for their pets, and make sure they're following your guidance. This is important with any kind of pet, including fish, hamsters, and reptiles. Keep cat and rabbit litter boxes extra-clean, hooded, and out of the way in the garage, bathroom, or a closet with a kitty door. If your pets live outdoors, they also need a clean, dry home and a place to exercise. Dog runs and horse stables need to be roomy and kept clean as well.

**Wildlife:** The Ch'i is enhanced in and around your home by inviting wild birds to visit your yard, balcony, or window. The more urban your domain, the more important this is. Our suburban yard includes three birdbaths, a small pond, a bird feeder, and a basket of peanuts. Two blue jays "own" the peanut basket, while a host of other birds bathe, eat, and cavort around the yard. Every year, the jays bring their babies here for peanut training. We also have two raccoons who visit several times a week to lounge in the pond. We provide these creatures with a sanctuary by leaving a portion of our yard in its natural state. As much as you can, bring nature with all its nourishing Ch'i close enough to your home to be enjoyed daily.

### *Mirrors*

Mirrors are a favorite Ch'i enhancement because they do such a good job of activating and circulating Ch'i throughout our homes. They bring light into dark areas, provide a sense of safety, and reflect beautiful views. They can also "cure" or erase architectural challenges such as poles, angles, and corners; as well as visually enlarge small spaces, such as hallways and foyers, which would otherwise feel very confining.

Because mirrors activate Ch'i, their presence makes a room more lively. This is wonderful in your living room, family room, home office, and kitchen. The bigger the mirror, the better! But mirrors can overstimulate rooms meant to be serene and relaxing, such as dining rooms and bedrooms.

**FIGURE 4N**

*This large mirrored closet effectively kept the bedroom "awake" all night, preventing a boy from getting a good night's sleep.*

**FIGURE 4O**

*A curtain that can be opened by day and closed at night solves the problem. Now the boy can have his mirrors and sleep, too.*

One of the quickest ways to calm a bedroom and its occupants is to remove or cover the mirrors. Large mirrors, like mirrored closet doors, can be treated as windows, with curtains or shades that open to bring in the daylight, and then close to quiet the room at night, as shown in Figures 4N and 4O. These photographs were taken in a teenage boy's bedroom. A month after the family moved into their new home, his mother noticed that he was sleeping with a light on at night. When she asked him why, he told her with some embarrassment that his room gave him the creeps. He would awaken in the middle of the night and feel like someone was in his room unless he left the light on. The "someone" was the wakeful Ch'i of the large mirrors. His mother made drapes that complemented his bed linens, and from the first night that the curtains were pulled across the mirrors, the creepy feeling disappeared, and he's slept peacefully ever since.

Other options are to cover the mirrored closet doors more permanently with fitted panels of cloth or wood, or to replace them with another type of door. You can also drape mirrors attached to bureaus with beautiful scarves or fabric in the evening and uncover them for daytime use. When you cannot see the door from the bed, a small mirror (or art with reflective glass), strategically hung to reflect the door is appropriate in the bedroom.

It is important to choose mirrors that reflect whole images. Clear, bright mirrors reflect clear, bright Ch'i. Therefore, mirrors that are one big, clear piece of glass are best. Beveling around the outside edges is fine, but fancy beveling that breaks up the mirror, foggy or broken antique mirrors, and mirrored tiles aren't recommended.

I found a large screen made of a dozen long, thin panels of beveled mirrors in my client Sally's home. Placed directly behind the living room sofa, it dominated the room. The room itself was beautiful, but the fractured images reflected in the mirror made me feel as if I were lost in a "house of mirrors." When I explained the mirror's effect, a big question was answered for Sally. She had wondered why her dates often ended so abruptly. She'd invite her beau in, they'd sit in the living room, and the next thing she knew, they were arguing. As a result, her love life always felt fractured. Sally immediately replaced the screen with one large mirror, reflecting one lovely image of the room. Within a month, she'd happily settled into one romantic relationship.

**FIGURE 4P** *(left)*

*This mirror is hung too low, cutting the top of this gentleman's head off and negatively affecting his self-image.*

**FIGURE 4Q** *(right)*

*He replaced the original mirror with a larger one, and hung it at the correct height so he can easily see his whole image.*

As shown in Figure 4Q, all of your mirrors should reflect your entire head, with several vertical inches to spare. Obviously, in a shared home, mirrors need to be large enough to reflect the heads of the shortest and the tallest adults in the house. (Tiny mirrors that are not used to reflect your image are an exception to this rule.) Seeing a full, clear image of yourself tends to enhance your self-esteem, whereas mirrors that cut your image off or into pieces, as in Figure 4P, have the opposite effect.

In one case, a client who had successfully overcome alcoholism began to drink again after he moved into a new home. In the bedroom he shared with his wife was a large mirror composed of many small beveled pieces that fractured his body's image every time he dressed. Because his wife's closet was in another room, she hadn't really noticed how disturbing it was to use his mirror. What's more, the mirror was hung low and cut off most of his head, presenting him with a bent and fractured image of himself every day. The couple replaced the offending mirror with serene art, and installed a large full-length wardrobe mirror inside the man's closet door. Less than two weeks after they made these changes, he was participating in a rehab program and has successfully returned to sobriety.

It's also important that your mirrors enhance the beauty and harmony in the room by reflecting a pleasant view. If you find a mirror reflecting an eyesore, either change the placement of the mirror or add a pleasing element that beautifies the reflection, and therefore, the room. Avoid hanging mirrors directly across from each other, as the endless reflections can be very disorienting.

In Feng Shui, small mirrors are sometimes used to reflect problems back to their source. If you have an unsightly view of power lines, sharp corners and angles from other buildings—or an impossible neighbor— you can hang a small mirror that faces *toward* the problem and directs it back from whence it came. This can be done outside a window or door with a disturbing view. Or, depending on the location of the problem, small mirrors can be placed behind a painting, under a rug, or on the ceiling. Often the mirror is not even seen once it's in place. Just remember to point the reflective side of the mirror toward the problem.

A mirror used in this way symbolically pushes the invasive energy back toward itself and draws a boundary between you and the offender. It's extremely important to imbue the mirror with your blessings and clear intention to improve the Ch'i. This is an act of clear boundary setting, not a curse. If your once-obnoxious neighbor suddenly moves or brings you cookies, you know that your mirror is working! Small mirrors used for this purpose can be purchased at Chinese specialty shops, or you can use compact mirrors found in cosmetic stores.

Mirrors symbolize self-image. Make it a daily practice to visualize yourself as radiantly happy, healthy, and prosperous. This practice steadily builds and strengthens your magnetism and sense of self. While mirrors can only show your reflection, your inner mirror reflects and upholds your spirit.

## *Nature Objects*

Creations of nature, such as rocks, pine cones, seed pods, driftwood, birds' nests, and shells, can be powerful, easy-care Ch'i enhancements. When endowed with personal meaning, these objects become sacred and can elicit potent memories of special times in nature. A beautiful rock found during a vacation will keep the memory of your mountain holiday alive for years to come. Pine cones gathered during a health retreat can symbolize vibrant health, while seashells found along the beach can hold the Ch'i of a magical moment when you felt completely relaxed and rejuvenated.

**FIGURE 4R**

*This collection of carved and polished gemstones symbolically holds the attributes of service, clarity, receptivity, love, and compassion in place, while strengthening the Wealth and Prosperity area of a work table.*

Nature objects can hold your goals, wishes, and aspirations in place. Figure 4R shows a collection of stones that symbolize attributes that the owner wants to keep in mind as she works. Arranged in the Wealth and Prosperity area of her work table, the collection is a reminder of life's abundant blessings.

I have a hickory nut that I found many years ago in the woods. At that time, I'd been looking for an apartment for weeks and had found nothing that suited my needs. Frustrated, I sat down under a huge hickory tree and prayed to be guided to the perfect place. Beside me on the ground was the hickory nut, and I picked it up as a symbol of my quest. That afternoon, with the nut in my pocket, I found the perfect apartment. To this day, it reminds me of how grateful I was to find a home.

Substantial objects of nature, such as boulders and logs, can also be incorporated into your home design. Rocks and boulders are considered great storehouses of natural energy, and they strengthen the Ch'i in any Bagua area. Logs, driftwood, or rocks can be incorporated into your furniture design or placed as either primary or accent garden pieces. Study their unique shapes and features, then position them so that their inspirational qualities are highlighted.

### Sound Makers

Sound makers summon and enhance Ch'i flow. Wind chimes, bells, bead curtains, musical instruments, gongs, and anything that makes a beautiful sound is considered a Ch'i enhancement. Always choose a resonant sound maker that lifts your spirits every time you hear it.

**FIGURE 4S**
*Wind chimes are classic enhancements that call in the Ch'i with their resonant tones. These chimes mark the Knowledge and Self-Cultivation corner of the house.*

The classic sound maker in Feng Shui is the wind chime, as seen in Figure 4S, which is often hung at the front door to call in positive energy. In her book, *Cultivating Sacred Space*, Elizabeth Murray says that wind chimes "draw music from the wind; a universal harmonic sound played spontaneously by nature." Wind chimes can be placed in any Bagua area you want to activate. Melodious sound makers also stimulate the energy in an area that feels claustrophobic and stagnant. They cleanse the space and return it to a more balanced, energized state, minimizing stress, illness, and lethargy. As sound makers, music and the sounds of nature can also be used to calm or energize a room and the people in it. Choose sounds—such as romantic, relaxing, or empowering music—that elicit the thoughts and feelings you want to experience.

**FIGURE 4T**

*The piano in this living room enhances the Children and Creativity area of the home. Displayed on the piano are photographs of children and friends. Original art by Lynn Hays was inspired by the garden surrounding the home.*

Sound makers can also enhance the feeling of safety by signaling a visitor's approach. The melodious sounds made by beaded curtains, bells, or chimes help define the boundaries between two areas, such as the living and dining rooms, or front entrances and foyers. All sound makers, including musical instruments such as guitars, flutes, and pianos (Figure 4T), can enhance the Ch'i in specific Bagua areas when they are appreciated and played regularly.

## Water Features

Water features attract and build vital Ch'i. Moving water, such as in fountains and waterfalls, encompasses both visual and auditory components and provides a pleasing place to rest the eye and the ear. A wide variety of interior and exterior fountains and waterfalls are available in every price range, or you can make your own (see bibliography for instruction booklet). Aquariums are considered excellent Ch'i enhancements, as they gather the Five Elements of Wood (plants), Fire (fish), Earth (sand), Metal (rocks), and Water into one dynamic feature.

**FIGURE 4U**

*A small water feature adorns an altar in a home sanctuary. Around the fountain are other Ch'i enhancements with personal meaning, including a framed quote and photograph, statue, shell candle, and inspirational books. The arrangement includes representations of each of the Five Elements.*

Adjust your water feature to sound like the natural murmur of a stream or waterfall—and not like a bathroom in use. Certain sounds of running water can be very distracting. For instance, a client had a dinner party shortly after installing a water fountain in her dining room. She noticed that no one could sit through the meal without excusing themselves to use the bathroom, including herself! She adjusted the sound of the fountain, and the need to run to the bathroom in the middle of dinner disappeared.

A water feature is often the centerpiece of an altar (as in Figure 4U) or a nature sanctuary. Many people have discovered that a small table fountain placed on their desk helps them to stay calm and centered throughout a hectic day. Fountains also add a wonderful welcoming presence in the foyer, as well as a calming sound in an infant's room. One enthusiastic client has a water feature in every room of her house, and she believes that each one enhances the abundant flow of work, rest, and play in her life.

Interior fountains, waterfalls, and aquariums are excellent choices for enhancing the Ch'i in any indoor Bagua area. They are considered especially powerful in the Wealth and Prosperity and Career areas because the element of water has a direct association with the abundant flow of money and resources.

Water features are also excellent choices for strengthening missing Bagua areas outside. Filling in where the corner or outside wall of the building is "missing," they symbolically complete the structure, while assuring the constant flow and circulation of Ch'i. In all cases, water features should flow *toward* the house, *into* the room, or 360 degrees around to correctly direct the energy.

All water features require regular cleaning and maintenance. Use distilled water in your interior fountains to greatly lengthen the time between cleanings. And be sure that nearby furniture and fabrics are not being damaged by splashing water.

Outdoor pools, Jacuzzis, and hot tubs are also considered water features, and must be kept clean, well lit, in good repair, and in many cases, fenced for safety. When choosing or designing these features, "amp" them up by including a waterfall flowing toward your house, and add enhancements such as beautiful landscaping, excellent lighting, and comfortable seating nearby.

As you are enjoying your water feature, remember that it symbolizes prosperity flowing into your life. Wealth comes in myriad forms—from the love you receive from family and friends, to the opportunities you have to grow and prosper. Count your blessings and write them down—bringing the unseen into the seen—and watch your blessings multiply.

### Wind Dancers

Wind dancers—such as mobiles, whirligigs, banners, prayer flags, and weather vanes—beckon, uplift, and invigorate Ch'i. Inside your home they can be used to lighten overhead beams, define and enhance rooms, and reinforce Bagua areas, as shown in Figure 4V.

**FIGURE 4V**

*This prayer flag by Geri Scalone gathers the colors of the Five Elements into one dynamic piece, while enhancing the Fame and Reputation area and draping the window of a meditation and healing room.* **(Also in color, page 116.)**

Wind dancers vary in size and can be made of just about anything. One client made a mobile with favorite greeting cards received from friends and hung it in the Health and Family area of her bedroom. When buying or making a wind dancer, choose lightweight materials if it will be hung over people's heads. Or, make your own wind dancer out of materials that hold special meaning for you, such as nature objects, photographs, or jewelry.

Outdoors, the movement and visual appeal of wind dancers attract and circulate Ch'i. As a friendly, memorable landmark in the front yard or near the front door, banners and flags highlight your home and direct energy into the house. A flag pole, banner, or whirligig can also be used to mark a missing Bagua area and symbolically complete a home's shape. A wind dancer such as a flag or whirligig can be suspended to visually correct and balance extreme conditions. Their color and movement raise heavy features such as eves and decks. Placed at the base of steep slopes, they lift the decline, while on the roof of a home built below street level, they elevate the structure.

Wind dancers are symbols of movement occurring from a solid base. They signify your ability to flow and change with the moment, and they can symbolize joy, creativity, or any other attribute that you want to unfurl and "catch the wind." Choose one that lifts your spirits as it captures the breeze.

*Chapter Five*

# THE FRONT ENTRANCE
# AND FOYER—
# A WELCOMING OPPORTUNITY

*"A seat, an armrest, a door handle which is comfortable
to hold, a terrace shaded from the heat, a flower growing
just along the entrance where I can bend down and smell
it as I pass . . . so that I know, with a small leap of the
heart, that I am back again . . ."*
— Christopher Alexander

Your front entrance—the area leading up to your front door, the threshold itself, and the area immediately inside the door—is important for two reasons. This is the area of first impressions, where *you*, your friends, neighbors, and community register immediate and lasting impressions about who you are. It is also the primary place through which vital energy enters your home. When open and welcoming, your front entrance communicates your desire and willingness to receive helpful experiences, people, and opportunities. When overgrown, poorly maintained, cluttered, or unpleasant, it says the opposite. Think of your front entrance as the avenue of good fortune that attracts helpful people and opportunities into your home. Roll out the welcome mat, and make it "entrancing."

### *An Entrancing Approach*

When designing your front entrance, include a meandering pathway to the front door that's wide enough to allow two people to approach side by side. The pathway should be distinct from the driveway, clear of obstacles and overgrown foliage, and well lit at night. An attractive gate,

**FIGURE 5A**

*To reach this home, one must cross a bridge into the enchanted world on the other side. Under the bridge runs a murmuring stream, complete with water-falls, koi fish, and water plants.* ***(Also in color, page 116.)***

arbor, or bridge can add interest and beauty to your design, as shown in Figure 5A. An outdoor water feature, either cool and still, or splashing nearby as in Figure 5C, can add a relaxing or opulent air. Let every season lend its own beauty to your front entrance, whether it's a riot of bright flowers, lush evergreens, or silvery succulents and herbs. Whatever form it takes, the beauty and grace of nature's offerings create the setting for the jewel that is your home. Add special touches and beauty marks such as outdoor seating, garden walls, statuary, nature objects, fragrant plants, and chimes.

**FIGURE 5B**

*A "clean slate," ready to be landscaped. Feng Shui guidelines help new owners decide how to appoint their front entrance.* ***(Also in color, page 117.)***

**FIGURE 5C**

*A large circular fountain accented with red geraniums enhances the Career area of home and property, with wide paths circling around the fountain to the front door. Two healthy evergreen "greeters" accented with seasonal flowers enhance either side of the front door.* ***(Also in color, page 117.)***

## A Celebratory Threshold

Make the color and design of your threshold area especially inviting so that you always feel welcomed home. In Feng Shui, red is traditionally included to attract prosperity and reasons to celebrate, so many people paint their front doors red. Although bright Chinese red is the classic favorite, any shade of red that's appealing to you is fine, including pink, terra-cotta, burgundy, purple, or magenta. Or choose a door that has artistic appeal, such as the one in Figure 5D, and accent the area around it with red, purple, or pink flowers; trees with red bark or berries; or planters, mats, and statuary in red tones. To enhance safety, the door or a nearby window should allow you to see who's there before opening it. Ideally, you can see out, but your visitor cannot see in until you've opened the door. Doors made primarily of glass can be curtained to assure privacy.

Even in the most humble or confined circumstances, a pot of bright flowers, wind chimes, or a seasonal wreath on the door can welcome you and your visitors home. If you cannot do anything outside your front door, as is often the case in apartment buildings, focus on making your interior foyer area welcoming and gracious.

**FIGURE 5D**

*Here, artist James Hubbell transforms a front door into a work of art. The door's stained glass provides owners with a view out, but visitors cannot see in. Red flowers and a gong (replacing the doorbell) further enhance the threshold area and attract Ch'i to the door.* ***(Also in color, page 118.)***

**FIGURE 5E**

*This foyer is located in the Knowledge and Self-Cultivation area of the house. The aquarium unites the Five Elements, while the standing Buddha statue and orchids represent inner wisdom and beauty. The fish in the original painting by Lynn Hays swim in a circle that opens to the right, subtly directing the flow of Ch'i into the living room.* **(Also in color, page 118.)**

## A Welcoming Foyer

Once inside the front door, an inviting foyer continues the welcoming embrace. Traditionally, the best painting in the house was hung in the foyer or near the front door as the "greeter," to honor guests and make a pleasing first impression. In one case, my first impression of a client was a large painting of a naked woman in her foyer. Although lovely, it was too intimate to be ideal as a greeter, so my client moved it to her bedroom. Interestingly enough, in her bedroom was a landscape that was perfect for the foyer! Whatever art you choose for your foyer, be sure it communicates an appropriately inviting message. In larger foyers, such as the one in Figure 5E, features such as an aquarium, carved statue, plant, furniture, lighting, or a water feature can be grouped together.

When your foyer is small, be careful not to overcrowd it in an effort to make it welcoming. Remove any furniture that impinges on the full use of front or closet doors, and choose a mirror or wall art with depth to make the foyer feel more spacious.

**FIGURE 5F**

*When standing in this threshold, we are greeted by the back of the couch and a few unrelated items on the far wall. Although a foyer space is somewhat defined by the couch, its back does not make a welcoming first impression, and those seated there have no view of the door.*

**FIGURE 5G**

*After applying Feng Shui principles, we are greeted by a red door and area rugs that guide us into the house. Shelves define a inviting foyer area and include a small fountain to enhance the Career area of the house. The shelves also provide a place for shoes in this "shoeless" home, as well as a basket of socks for guests. An attractive arrangement of greeters, including a vase by Alex Long and a painting by Louise Hoffman, have been grouped on the far wall to welcome people and draw energy into the room.*

No matter how small your foyer area is, carve out a token place of welcome. Even if you have no official foyer, arrange your furniture to suggest one, and place symbols of welcome near the front door, as shown in Figure 5G. Do whatever you can to present your guests—and yourself—with a warm and welcoming first impression.

Keep the indoor foyer clear of migrating possessions such as toys, sports equipment, recyclables, and mail. Give these items homes in nearby closets and furniture. Also consider making your home a shoeless house. Design a place near the front door to store shoes, and have socks or slippers available for guests. This helps to keep your home clean, and symbolizes leaving your worldly cares at the door.

Whatever your tastes and preferences in colors, styles, and design, give your whole front entrance area the attention necessary to make it as beautiful and welcoming as you can. In so doing, you will attract a cornucopia of great relationships and experiences into your life.

### Doubling Your Enchantment with the Bagua Map

The Bagua Map (Chapter 2) can make your foyer enhancements doubly meaningful (see Figures 5E and 5G). When your front entrance is unsightly, chaotic, or in any way unpleasant, it affects the quality of your life. For instance, a very successful writer who had experienced tremendous success noticed that career opportunities had waned considerably over the last few months. Her front door was recessed so that the Career area included the front pathway and patio of her home, which were crowded with spiky foliage and pots of dead and dying plants. The tattered screen door was partially blocked by more sad plants and rusty garden tools. The whole setting clearly indicated how she had put the brakes on her career.

When she realized that her parched and thorny front entrance symbolized her current lack of opportunities, she gave the patio a complete makeover, adding wind chimes, healthy plants, outdoor furniture, and a water fountain that, as she put it, brought some "juiciness" to her front entrance. She also fixed the screen door and painted the front door a rich shade of violet. Inside, she defined a welcoming foyer area with a table, lamp, flowers, and an inspirational quote she had written and published.

Within a week, exciting opportunities began to pour in the door, including the chance to host her own television show. By upgrading her front entrance, she had rejuvenated her career.

### *What You See Is What You Get*

Whatever room you see first when entering your front door tends to set the focus for the whole house. The living room is considered very good because it suggests social interaction and relaxation. When the first room sighted is the kitchen, dining room, bedroom, bathroom, or laundry room, it can put the focus of the house on other activities such as eating, sleeping, and doing chores.

If you live in a home like this, you can rearrange furniture or add screens so that these aren't the first rooms you see. For instance, a couple's dining room was the first room they saw from the front entrance. Their biggest complaint was that they'd both gained unwanted pounds since they'd moved in a year before. They snacked continually while at home and could not stay on any reasonable diet. When they realized that dining was the focus of the house, they reversed the dining room and the den. Now, when they come home, they enter the den, which promotes relaxation and conversation rather than food consumption, and they enjoy a dining room that's located away from the front door.

When we are first greeted by a bedroom or bathroom, the best thing to do is keep the door to the room closed. Neither toilets nor beds make ideal first impressions. Put each door on a soft spring so that it closes gently and easily behind you. Enhance the door itself by appointing it with a mirror or favorite textile.

Another Feng Shui challenge is seeing multiple rooms from the foyer. This can be disorienting to new visitors and occupants alike. In these cases, it's important to highlight one room, such as the living room, by laying a clear path to it with the artful use of screens, sculpture, art, plants, and furniture placement. For instance, a decorative screen placed to partially obscure a dining room entrance can lead people directly into the living room. Or, a sculpture that includes light or movement in the living room will draw people's attention directly into that room.

## *Upgrading All Entrances*

The front door to your home is considered the primary mouth of Ch'i, even when you often use another entrance. If the entrance you most often use opens into a laundry room, hall, or stairwell, make sure it's welcoming, well lit, and completely accessible. Be sure you are greeted by beauty and light, not darkness and clutter, so that the first and last impression of your own home is a good one. One favorite poster in the laundry room or elegant tapestry in a stairwell can make all the difference in how welcome you feel arriving home. Some people turn these areas into fun art galleries, displaying photographs, collages, and personal mementos that don't fit in other areas of the house. Others include elegant possessions near their everyday entrance, such as an oil painting or gilt-framed mirror. Whatever you choose, your enhancements are indeed well placed when they welcome you home.

### Quick Reference Guidelines for the Front Entrance

- Create an "entrancing" front entrance area, inside and out.
- Keep the entire area safely lit, well maintained, and clutter-free.
- In outdoor areas, include meandering paths, water features, seating, and other "beauty marks."
- Indoors, display one or more welcoming "greeters" in the foyer or the area just inside the front door.
- Embellish the foyer area according to the Bagua Map.
- Enhance other entrances that are used often.

# Chapter Six

# THE LIVING ROOM—
# SHARING WHO YOU
# ARE WITH THE WORLD

*"An interior is the natural projection of the soul."*
— Coco Chanel

**FIGURE 6A**

*Yin and Yang find balance in this living room, which includes comfortable, well-placed seating and rounded tables made by artist Brett Hesser.* ***(Also in color, page 118.)***

The living room, such as the one shown in Figure 6A, is well placed as the first room you enter from the foyer. Because it is a social, active room, the living room is associated with the Fire element in Feng Shui. It's the perfect place to "put yourself out there" and display the art, colors, and collections that you love. Living rooms speak volumes about your personality and how you view the world, so make it an accurate account. Here, the focus is to express your individuality in any design style that suits you, while arranging your furnishings and treasures to assure harmonious Ch'i flow.

### Living in Comfort and Safety

As described in Chapter 1, comfort and safety are important when furnishing your living room. Buy only the seating that embraces you in its comfortable arms, and furniture that is free of annoying or dangerous detailing. Furniture that catches or "bites" toes or clothing, and seating that offers no support have no place in your home. Tables with sharp corners can be dangerous, and energetically, they push people and Ch'i away rather than drawing them in—especially when pointing toward doors or seating. If you have living room tables and chairs with sharp angles or corners, unsafe detailing, or protruding legs, they need to be softened, repositioned, or replaced. Use fabric, table runners, plants, or other items to soften them or turn the piece at a diagonal to position corners away from people.

When shopping for new furniture, make safety and comfort just as important as beauty. Look for designs with friendly detailing and rounded corners, even when the overall shape is rectangular. Because every body is different, be sure to actually "test drive" sofas and chairs before purchasing them. An item may look good in a brochure or magazine, but your body will tell you if it's really right for you.

### Minding the View

To encourage social intimacy and relaxation, place the primary piece of living room furniture—often a sofa—so that it commands a view of the door, as shown in Figure 6B. When this is not possible, hang a mirror so that the door's reflection can be seen from the sofa. Once your primary furniture is placed, give other seating a full, partial, or mirror view of the door if at all possible. This attention to the view from every seat goes a long way toward putting everyone at ease and making the room both attractive and comfortable. To increase the sense of comfort and good Ch'i flow, arrange your living room furniture to form islands that you can move around easily.

**FIGURE 6B**

*In this living room, everyone, including the family pet, has a view of the door. Notice the rounded shapes on the sofa, chair, and coffee table. Artist Karen Haughey's painting enhances the Health and Family area of the room, while the piano, lamp, and photos of loved ones anchor the Wealth and Prosperity area.*

Check the view from every seat in the living room, and correct any eyesores. To assure ideal views and energy flow throughout the room, make sure the corners in your living room are clear of clutter. Appoint corners with any combination of enhancements, such as plants, sculpture, lighting, and furniture—or soften with fabric.

**FIGURE 6C**

*The mirror above the fireplace strikes a dynamic balance between the Fire and Water elements, while bringing more light into the room.*

An archetypal symbol of comfort and safety, the fireplace is well placed in a living room. Sometimes, however, its size and location dominates the room. When this is the case, you can draw from the Five Elements (Chapter 3) and introduce the Water element to balance the Fire. One very popular way to do this is to hang a mirror representing Water over the fireplace, as shown in Figure 6C, and in Figure 4H on page 76. Water can also be introduced via paintings of oceans, lakes, streams, and rivers, or artwork with a free-form or asymmetrical design. Objects made of black or very dark-colored materials, as well as crystal and glass items, also symbolize the Water element. A glass screen in front of the fireplace, crystal vases on the mantel, or a water feature near the fireplace are all ways you can introduce Water and balance Fire.

### *Too Much of a Good Thing*

Many living rooms are populated with an overwhelming number of decorative items. When asked to help identify why a couple's home wasn't selling, I found more than a hundred stunning crystal pieces in the living room. They were lined up on glass shelves, making the room look more like a fine crystal store than a living space. The sight of so many glittering objects did more to push me out of the room than to invite me in, which, according to the real estate agent, happened to prospective buyers, too. For most people, the sheer volume of crystal on display was simply too much. Because the couple wanted to keep their entire collection, our solution was to take a third of their collection, spread it throughout the house, and pack the rest. With the experience of too much becoming just right, their house sold almost immediately.

Many people believe that to practice Feng Shui they'll have to embrace the "Zen," or minimalist look, and that's just not true. Feng Shui and material abundance are not mutually exclusive! Feng Shui is always striving for the perfect balance between extremes, and each of us has a different opinion about what constitutes too much or too little. If you have so many things that displaying them all would be too much, rotate your collections, displaying some of them and storing the rest. This gives each of your treasures a chance to shine without having to share the stage with hundreds of other "lovelies."

Pillows can also overpopulate a living room. Many homes have so many pillows on the couches and chairs that all the seating appears to be taken. Pillows are meant to accent your furniture and give back support to the people sitting there. Any more is too much of a good thing. When accenting with pillows, choose designs that are wear-worthy, meaning that they're not so fancy as to be damaged by use.

Consider your pillows and other beautiful curios as jewelry for your living room. You may have a huge collection, but the living room doesn't need to "wear" every one of them all the time. Dress your living room in a selection of your beautiful things, as you would appoint an outfit with jewelry and other accessories. Then change them as you like, storing your extras in "jewelry boxes," or places where you can easily select them as needed. This assures good Ch'i flow throughout your living room and the pleasure of rediscovering and enjoying all the belongings you love.

---

### CONTEMPLATIVE EXERCISE

IMAGINE LIVING WITHOUT YOUR COLLECTIONS. ARE YOU ABLE TO REMAIN CONNECTED TO YOUR SENSE OF HAPPINESS, ABUNDANCE, AND INSPIRATION? BY THEIR VERY NATURE, POSSESSIONS COME AND GO, WHILE YOUR INNER QUALITIES BECOME MORE MAGNIFICENT WITH TIME. YOUR GREATEST COLLECTION, AND THE ONE THAT WILL INCREASE IN VALUE OVER A LIFETIME, IS YOUR COLLECTION OF INNER RESOURCES AND POSITIVE CHARACTER TRAITS. DECIDE WHAT ATTRIBUTE YOU COULD ADD TO THE COLLECTION YOU'LL BE LIVING WITH FOR A LIFETIME.

---

## Chatty Cabinets

While writing *Home Design with Feng Shui A–Z*, I had a very interesting experience. Our home has a wall of built-in cabinets in the living room where we store much of our house "jewelry." One cabinet is reserved for ornamental items such as vases, decorative boxes, and candleholders. I happened to open that cabinet after a day of writing about how our possessions talk to us whenever we're around them. What I saw when I opened the cabinet was not a number of pretty things, but a crowd of people. Each item evoked a memory of a person that I probably wouldn't have remembered for any other reason—some of them great, some of them not so great. And, for a moment in time, those people were sitting on my shelf talking to me.

One voice came from a hand-painted wooden box that I'd bought for a friend years ago and had never given her. I liked it, bought her something else, and kept the box for myself. Still, the box seemed to have her name written on it. So there she sat, reminding me yet again to give her the box. I felt the same stab of guilt I experienced every time I looked at it. Sitting next to "her" was a pencil holder my grandfather had carved from a piece of firewood. There he proudly sat on my shelf, telling me that he could make something beautiful out of just about anything. Each "person" had something to say, and for the first time, I really took the time to listen. As a result, I finally gave my friend (who loved my story about the "talking" cabinet) her wooden box, and put my grandfather's pencil holder on my desk. I also let go of a number of chatty items that, although beautiful, didn't belong in the crowd of memories I like to hang out with. Now when I open that cabinet, the voices I hear are sweet and elicit wonderful feelings and memories.

---

## CONTEMPLATIVE EXERCISE

WE'VE ALL HEARD THE SAYING "SKELETONS IN YOUR CLOSET." IT BECOMES QUITE LITERAL IN FENG SHUI. TAKE A LOOK AT YOUR "HOUSE JEWELRY," AND SORT OUT THE THINGS THAT EVOKE UNPLEAS- ANT MEMORIES, FEELINGS, OR ASSOCIATIONS. LISTEN TO THE TALE EACH ITEM HAS TO TELL, AND DECIDE IF YOU REALLY WANT IT IN YOUR SPACE. STEP FULLY INTO THE PRESENT, YOUR PLACE OF POWER, AND LET GO OF ANYTHING THAT DOESN'T HAVE NICE THINGS TO SAY. IN SO DOING, YOUR ENERGY, AS WELL AS THE ENERGY IN YOUR ENVIRONMENT, WILL SOAR.

---

### Colors of Our Lives

Color is a personal and powerful tool for enhancing your home. A previous owner may have loved dusty pink rose wallpaper or avocado green walls, while you find yourself feeling claustrophobic or nauseated by those patterns and colors. Make it a high priority to remove offensive colors, and surround yourself with the colors that feed and nurture you.

Your color scheme can be entirely neutral, or a variety of subtle or intense shades. Just remember that you can't change the color of your living room as easily as your wardrobe. You'll be living with your color choices for a while. This isn't to suggest that you should be timid with color—just smart.

Experiment before ordering colorful paint, upholstery, or furniture. Before buying a purple chair, for example, drape purple paper or fabric where the chair would go, and live with it for a week or so. Brightly colored furnishings, walls, or floors might look good in someone else's home or in designer magazines, but test the color before diving in.

Observe how light interacts with the color you could be living with morning, noon, and night. Many colors look completely different in natural light than in artificial light. Make sure you like all the moods and tones your color choices bring into your home. If you live with others, find out if they like the color. If you're less enamored with the color by the end of the week, try another one and be grateful you found out before you made a big investment.

When chosen well, colors add a powerful, healing quality to your home. And, because you are always changing, the colors you've chosen for your home will need to change from time to time to reflect your new self. Neutral or subtle tones in your wall, carpet, and sofa colors are often recommended, as they give you the freedom to accessorize in a variety of colors that can be changed as often as you like.

There are other ways you can use color to enhance your environment. Using the controlling cycle of the Five Elements (Chapter 3), colors can be used as a "quick fix" when a room appears to be too monochromatic for your taste. Choose reds and purples to warm up an environment that is primarily white. Introduce yellows and earthtones to balance rooms that contain a lot of black or very dark colors. Add white and very light pastels to an environment that's too blue or green. And dark colors and black help to balance an overabundance of fiery colors, such as red or purple.

Another effective way of using color to enhance your home is to group items that include all the colors of the Five Elements together. Multicolored fabrics, paintings, collectibles, and candles (Figure 18A, page 128) offer endless possibilities.

You can use color when enhancing the Ch'i in the different areas of the Bagua Map (Chapter 2), but only use the associated colors when you find them appealing. Do not feel pressured to use black in your Career Gua, or red in your Fame and Reputation Gua unless you are personally attracted to these colors. Colors enhance the Ch'i only if they lift and inspire you each time you see them.

**FIGURE 2I**

*This is a view of the home's Love and Marriage area, a footprint drawing of which appears in Figure 2B, page 26, taken shortly after the new owners moved in.*

**FIGURE 2J**

*To anchor the Love and Marriage area, the couple chose to plant an olive tree, symbolizing strength and longevity of love. A large built-in planter and flower border further accent the area. They also added outdoor living areas to both floors, enhancing the beauty and functionality of the area.*

**FIGURE 3B**

*This inviting foyer arrange-
ment includes all the elements.
The flower arrangement represents Wood; the large red flowers and small birds add Fire;
the rectangular shape and
detailing of the mirror bring in
Earth; the half-circular table
and white bowl capture Metal;
and the mirror, representing
water, completes the elemental
arrangement.*

**FIGURE 4A**

*Art can be chosen to
enhance specific Bagua
areas in the home.
This painting of vibrant
flowers by Monte
deGraw strengthens
health and vitality in
the Health and Family
area located in the
living room.*

**FIGURE 4B**

*When the Health and Family area is in the bedroom, the art you choose may be different. Jeff Kahn's painting of two vibrantly healthy people is more intimate and fits well into a bedroom.*

**FIGURE 4J**

*During the summer months, this fireplace becomes a "candleplace." Sand covers the floor of the fireplace, supporting various arrangements of candles and holders throughout the warm season.*

**FIGURE 4V** (*left*)

*This prayer flag by Geri Scalone gathers the colors of the Five Elements into one dynamic piece, while enhancing the Fame and Reputation area and draping the window of a meditation and healing room.*

**FIGURE 5A** (*below*)

*To reach this home, one must cross a bridge into the enchanted world on the other side. Under the bridge runs a murmuring stream, complete with waterfalls, koi fish, and water plants.*

**FIGURE 5B**

*A "clean slate," ready to be landscaped. Feng Shui guidelines help new owners decide how to appoint their front entrance.*

**FIGURE 5C**

*A large circular fountain accented with red geraniums enhances the Career area of home and property, with wide paths circling around the fountain to the front door. Two healthy evergreen "greeters" accented with seasonal flowers enhance either side of the front door.*

**FIGURE 5D**

*Here, artist James Hubbell transforms a front door into a work of art. The door's stained glass provides owners with a view out, but visitors cannot see in. Red flowers and a gong (replacing the doorbell) further enhance the threshold area and attract Ch'i to the door.*

**FIGURE 5E**

*This foyer is located in the Knowledge and Self-Cultivation area of the house. The aquarium unites the Five Elements, while the standing Buddha statue and orchids represent inner wisdom and beauty. The fish in the original painting by Lynn Hays swim in a circle that opens to the right, subtly directing the flow of Ch'i into the living room.*

**FIGURE 6A**

*Yin and Yang find balance in this living room, which includes comfortable, well-placed seating and rounded tables made by artist Brett Hesser.*

**FIGURE 7A**

*This round dining table is the perfect size for two people to enjoy a meal together. Candles and table linens warm the stone and metal table, while comfortable chairs add the finishing touch. Art by Lynn Hays adds color and vibrancy, while flowers soften and enhance the corner.*

**FIGURE 10A**

*This was the home office of a marketing consultant before improvements. His back was to the door, and the room was very disorganized. The Fire element, seen in the red chair, fiery rug, and large tiger painting, dominated the room. This correlated with the man's ongoing problems involving volatile and unpleasant clients.*

**FIGURE 10B**

*Improvements included repositioning the desk to command the room and provide a view of the door. The desk's frosted glass, black supports, black computer mat, and crystal bowl represent the cooling influence of the Water element. The fiery rug was removed to correct the overabundance of the Fire element and improve movement of the desk chair. Filing and other organizational systems were designed to match the man's style and keep him organized. Soon after these changes were made, he was given an ongoing full-time project by his favorite client.*

**FIGURE 11A**

*This bedroom includes warm colors, soft linens, favorite art, and an overall simple and serene design.*

**FIGURE 11Q**

*This bedroom, although appealing in many ways, holds a woman's single status in place. The single horse is perpetually galloping away in the Love and Marriage area of the room. The doll and delicate pillows "protect" the bed, and suggest that it's already taken. The teddy bear in the chair, the single-woman statue on the bureau, the "one night stand," and the lamp all symbolize aloneness. And the white gauzy curtain suggests that bandages are needed for injuries from past love affairs.*

**FIGURE 11R**

*The bedroom is now inviting romance. Delicate pillows, the doll, teddy bear, horse, statue, and gauze curtain have been removed. Candles, flowers, a second nightstand and lamp, deep red linens, and an area rug have been added. Best of all, the Love and Marriage area is now enhanced with a sensual sculpture by Ert'e.*

**FIGURE 11S**

*Sensual sculpture by Ert'e brings an air of romance into the bedroom.*

**FIGURE 11T**

*This single man's bedroom includes many Feng Shui challenges, including bed placement, exercise equipment, bedside art of a lonely man, one lamp and night-stand, a partner-eating plant, and a general lack of order. The large white painting by Richard Haeger is lost in a white room dominated by the Metal element.*

**FIGURE 11U**

*Changes include moving the bed to a solid wall, adding a colorful painting by Sally Pearce, red rugs, and a second nightstand and lamp. Luxurious linens warm up the bed, while a red candle, a table by Charles Thomas, and sculpture by Karin Swildens enhance the Love and Marriage area. A healthy new palm accents the Wealth and Prosperity area.*

**FIGURE 13A**

*Many Ch'i enhancements including red walls, a plant, art, luxurious tow-els, and a low-wattage lamp that's always on keep the Ch'i buoyant in this windowless bathroom.*

**FIGURE 17D**

*Arrange intimate views with beauty marks, such as this angel birdbath and seasonal flowers outside the home office, kitchen, bedroom, and bathroom windows.*

**FIGURE 18A**

*These candles have been grouped together to represent the Five Elements and to cleanse and purify the energy in the room.*

### *Controlling the Wild Electronic Beast*

Locate televisions and other electronic equipment in cabinets with doors so they can be concealed when not in use. This one simple ad ment can dramatically improve the quality of life by promoting a variety of social and family activities, as well as times of peace and calm.

One couple's large television sat on an open shelf in their living room. When I suggested that they store it in a cabinet or armoire, they were a little bit taken aback. Most of their friends' televisions were on full display, and the bigger, the better! Why should they hide theirs? I suggested that they experiment and simply cover the TV with an attractive cloth between uses for a couple of weeks. After that time, they could decide whether it had made a difference in the quality of their lives.

Two weeks later, they were out shopping for a TV cabinet with doors. They had discovered that, when the TV was not in plain view, they watched it less. For them, the best part was that the temptation to eat "in front of the tube" had greatly diminished. Now, instead of TV newscasters joining them every night for dinner, they joined each other to catch up on the day. In doing so, they relaxed more and experienced indigestion less. Months later, their discovery had spread to many of their friends, who were also putting their televisions behind closed doors.

### *Ceilings—Heaven and Earth in Place*

Ceilings vary greatly in height, depending on the age and style of the house. Feng Shui addresses the fact that most people prefer to live under a ceiling that is neither too low nor too high, usually about eight to ten feet. When too much higher or lower, the room becomes less inviting to relax in. If your living room, or any other room, has a particularly low or high ceiling, there are ways you can make the room feel more comfortable.

**<u>Low Ceilings:</u>** One of the most effective ways to balance a room with a low ceiling is with lighting that shines *up* toward the ceiling. You can also paint the ceiling white or a light pastel, which will lift the perceived height of the ceiling, especially when your up-lights are on.

Use light and bright colors throughout the room, mirrors when appropriate, and as little dark color as possible. Low furnishings keep the room in scale and make the ceiling appear higher. Because a low ceiling is considered Yin, rooms with low ceilings are best for Yin purposes, such as bedrooms or sanctuaries for yoga and meditation.

**FIGURE 6D**

*The ceiling in this living room is more than 15 feet high. To "draw the line between heaven and earth," paintings by the owner were hung at the same height to draw a strong horizontal line around the room. Shelves further define the "earth" portion of the room.*

**High Ceilings:** Many Western homes include high ceilings in the living, dining, or bedroom areas. Although considered architecturally dramatic, a high ceiling can be too "heavenly" or Yang and make the room feel more like a grand gallery or theater than a cozy, comfortable place to live. High ceilings tend to pull people "up and out" of themselves, which, in public buildings, can be great. At home, however, most people like to be "down and in," where they can kick back, relax, and restore their energy.

To balance the high ceiling's abundance of Yang Ch'i, you can "draw the line between heaven and earth," a Feng Shui term for drawing a strong horizontal line around the room. This line defines where the horizontal "earth" of the living space ends, and the vertical "heaven" of the high ceiling begins. When a line clearly defines the cozy earth below and the heavenly spheres above, the room becomes much more attractive and comfortable.

The line between heaven and earth can be drawn around the room using crown molding, wainscoting, stenciling (Figure 11M, page 183), wallpaper, or shelving six to ten feet above the floor. One way to choose the exact height is to use the top of a large piece of furniture, or a door or window jamb as your guide. The materials used can be the same color as the walls to subtly suggest the line, or you can decorate the walls differently above and below the line with different colors, wallpapers, or wall textures. When installing a shelf for this purpose, be sure to accent it only with lightweight objects, such as baskets, textiles, or silk plants.

A line can also be visually suggested by hanging your art at the same height around the room, as shown in Figure 6D. The eye will then "fill in the blanks." As with wainscoting, you can hang your art at the same height as the tops of furniture, windows, and doors so that the combined effect draws a strong horizontal line around the room. Hang large art pieces so that the tops of the frames are all at the same height, or group smaller art pieces together to achieve the same effect. In one instance, a little-used living room became the favorite spot in the house after the residents hung all their art at the same height around the room. Their simple adjustment grounded the room and gave it enough definition to make it a comfortable place to be.

In some cases, the line can be drawn by building a loft into a room to create two cozy places that may suit your needs far better than one vertically spacious room. Canopied fabrics can also draw a strong horizontal line to create intimate nooks. Be creative, and work with the room until you are very comfortable there.

Consider embellishing the heavenly space above the line with "sky art," or items that define the heavens above, and add an inspirational quality to the room. A sparkling crystal chandelier suspended over a table is a classic example. When choosing items for this purpose, be sure that they aren't hung over seating or are at least lightweight, such as banners, mobiles, or textiles. The visual strength of your line between heaven and earth, as well as the possible addition of heavenly art above, gives high-ceilinged rooms the interest and coziness they need to be comfortable for everyday living.

Ceilings that are vaulted on only one side also need a strong horizontal line drawn to balance the difference in ceiling heights. Follow the previous instructions on drawing the line between heaven and earth to bring the room into balance.

### Beams—Lightening the Load

Beams are a popular structural feature in Western architecture, and they are often thought to add character to a room. They can also add a disturbing sense of heaviness overhead, especially when you sit or sleep directly under them. The bigger, darker, and lower the beams are, the more ominous they can seem; while smaller, lighter, and higher beams are less of a problem. Therefore, we want to lighten and lift large, dark, or low beams, diminishing the uncomfortable weight-of-the-world feeling overhead.

**FIGURE 6E**

*The beam in this living room has been balanced with the classic Feng Shui enhancement of bamboo flutes. Many other enhancements complement the room, including candles, plants, flowers, art, an aquarium, and of course, Garfield the cat.*

Blend beams with the ceiling by painting or staining them to match the ceiling color. Painting them white or a very light pastel color will make them appear lighter. Beams are also softened by adding curves that suggest an arch at either end, or they can be "lifted" with the artful use of lighting. Install strings of tiny white lights along the beams, or use up-lighting to lift them from below.

In traditional Feng Shui, two bamboo flutes were hung on the beam at 45-degree angles to symbolically break the beam's dominant influence in the room (Figure 6E). These flutes were hung with the mouthpieces down to symbolize the music flowing up to lift the beam. In Western homes, we can replace bamboo flutes with any type of wood pieces, or subtly suggest these angled lines by painting them onto the beams.

Other objects that "lighten up" beams, whether real or artistically suggested, include feathers, floral swags, vines, birds, and angels. Or hang beautiful lightweight prayer flags, silk banners, or mobiles from the beam. Always choose things that are actually light, so as not to add to the burdensome feeling of heaviness overhead. (Beams are also softened by adding curves that suggest an arch at each end.)

### Making the Most of Your Living Room

As you're working with your living room, keep the Bagua Map (Chapter 2) and the Five Elements (Chapter 3) in mind. There are myriad ways to energize your living room using these two systems. As an example, art in a living room located in the Children and Creativity area may be chosen for its playful and colorful qualities, while art in a living room located in Health and Family may portray radiantly healthy people, or gardens and forests.

Each of the Five Elements should have a presence in your living room—*how* is up to you. You may choose to rely on color, or literally bring the elements in via plants, candles, ceramics, metal art, and a water feature. You could also choose to subtly balance the elements with wooden tables (Wood), animal statuary (Fire), tiled floors (Earth), round pillows (Metal), and a mirror (Water). There is no end to the unique combinations you can put together. Be guided by what you love, and enjoy the results.

---

### CONTEMPLATIVE EXERCISE

TAKE A FEW MOMENTS TO SIT QUIETLY IN YOUR LIVING ROOM. LOOK AROUND AND DETERMINE IF THE ROOM PROVIDES AN ACCURATE REFLECTION OF WHO YOU ARE. IF YOU LIVE WITH OTHER PEOPLE, CONSIDER WHETHER YOUR LIVING ROOM REFLECTS A HARMONIOUS BLEND OF EVERYONE'S TASTES AND INTERESTS. NOTE WHETHER YOU ARE COMFORTABLE WITH WHAT YOU SEE AND HOW YOU FEEL IN THE ROOM. IF THERE ARE FEATURES THAT YOU FIND DISCONCERTING, DECIDE WHAT YOU NEED TO DO NOW TO CORRECT THEM. YOU MAY NEED TO TALK WITH A SPOUSE ABOUT RELOCATING A PAINTING, STRIKE A COMPROMISE WITH A ROOMMATE, HAVE A PIECE OF FURNITURE REUPHOLSTERED, DISPLAY A CHERISHED MEMENTO, CHANGE THE ARRANGEMENT OF FURNITURE, OR CLEAN OUT A CLUTTERED CORNER. WHATEVER IT IS, MAKE YOUR LIVING ROOM AS ACCURATE AN EXPRESSION OF YOU AS POSSIBLE—A PLACE WHERE YOU REALLY ENJOY SPENDING TIME.

---

#### QUICK REFERENCE GUIDELINES FOR THE LIVING ROOM

- Express yourself and show the world who you are.
- Arrange your furniture to improve Ch'i flow.
- Situate your primary piece of furniture, such as your sofa, so that it has a view of the door.
- Eliminate or soften sharp corners and angles.
- Strike a "just right" balance with the number of decorative items you display.
- Look before you leap into your color scheme.
- Choose furnishings that are safe and comfortable, as well as beautiful.
- Open up and enhance the corners in the room.
- Put the TV and other electronic equipment behind closed doors.
- Balance ceiling heights and heavy beams.
- Take the Bagua Map and the Five Elements into consideration.

# Chapter Seven

# THE DINING ROOM— NURTURING BODY, HEART, AND SOUL

*"Dining is, and always was, a great artistic opportunity."*
— Frank Lloyd Wright

**FIGURE 7A**

*This round dining table is the perfect size for two people to enjoy a meal together. Candles and table linens warm the stone and metal table, while comfortable chairs add the finishing touch. Art by Lynn Hays adds color and vibrancy, while flowers soften and enhance the corner.* **(Also in color, page 119.)**

## *Reclaiming the Ritual of Dining*

The dining room—what a wonderful place to linger over breakfast and read the paper; to sit back during lunch and daydream for a while; and to relax, refuel, and enjoy conversation over dinner. Sound like a typical day in your dining room? Most of my clients say they rarely have these experiences. In many homes, the dining table and chairs remain empty most of the time. Some homes don't have a dining room per se, but rather a dining *place*, such as a nook or an area within a larger room in which to dine. Whether it's a dining place or a dining room, chances are it's not used often.

In Feng Shui, the dining room is related to the Earth element. It is the place to partake of the bounty of the earth and replenish our bodies with life-sustaining Ch'i. Our cultural tendency is to rush through meals, pounding our food down while perched at the kitchen counter; or eating while standing, driving, or watching television. Fast food of every description serves our eat-on-the-run lifestyle, while endless distractions require us to hurry and eat faster. The trouble is, as the fine art of dining is relegated to the occasional special event, we are starving ourselves energetically. By taking the time to eat slowly and thoughtfully, we are receiving the full vitality of our food, and in every way, nurturing ourselves.

## *A Nourishing Atmosphere*

Like the couple seen in Figure 7A, make it a point to create an atmosphere conducive to dining—a place that has its own intimate, peaceful atmosphere. Because nourishment is so vital to our health and well-being, Feng Shui encourages us to design a pleasant and serene dining environment. Turn off the telephone, play soft music, set the table, light candles, and dine at a leisurely pace. Arrange furniture, plants, area rugs, and other Ch'i enhancements to define and appoint a dining room that supports reflection, digestion, and intimate conversation. The more hectic your days are, the more important the ritual of dining is to your health and happiness. Such a place slows you down enough to become aware of the Ch'i qualities in your food. And, it attunes you to the essential vitality that is being passed to you in every meal. You also receive the invaluable gift of connecting with yourself and other people who may be breaking bread with you. Make your dining room an oasis where you can nourish both the body and the spirit.

### A Delicious Chair

Because comfort is so important, ergonomics—the study of the human body's physiostructural needs—plays a very important role in Feng Shui. Dining chairs, when ergonomically correct, hold your body comfortably and invite you to relax. Unfortunately, there are many types of chairs on the market that are ergonomically incorrect, negatively affecting the body's structural alignment and vitality, as well as dining enjoyment. These kinds of chairs are considered the "high heels" of furniture. As beautiful as they may look, they are uncomfortable and ungrounding to "wear" for any length of time. Like high-heeled shoes, they can easily deplete your Ch'i rather than enhance it.

No matter how cute, expensive, or stylish dining chairs are, they need to pass the safety and comfort test to serve their function. They should be stable and support your weight without folding up or falling over. Chairs with protruding legs, or decorative backs that poke or cut you should be left on the showroom floor. Look for chairs with well-formed, padded, or upholstered seats, and backs that embrace the contours of your body. This means that most wooden, plastic, and metal chairs need to be cushioned to be comfortable. Make sure all your dining chairs are equally comfortable, which shows your desire to make everyone feel honored and welcome (Figure 7B). Avoid the "king and queen" chairs that communicate inequality and leave other diners to sit in less comfortable seats, as in Figure 7C. Just like shoes, dining chairs that are both sensible and beautiful do the best job in supporting a nourishing flow of energy in the dining room.

Always *sit* in a chair before buying it. When shopping for chairs, take a book with you, and when you find a chair you like, sit in it for a while to be sure your body likes it. No matter how perfect a chair looks in a brochure or catalog, it can't pass the safety and comfort test until you actually sit in it. Once you've decided that you like the feel of a chair, *then* decide whether you like the look of it. If you do, the chair's a keeper, and another very discerning Feng Shui shopper has been satisfied.

**FIGURE 7B**

*This dining room demonstrates excellent Feng Shui. All the chairs are very comfortable, conveying an equality that honors all diners. The rounded corners and general design of the table pose no danger. A prized collection of silver, plants, and other appointments have been chosen to create a pleasant, tranquil place to dine. Although this furniture happens to be of oriental design, any style can be chosen to meet Feng Shui guidelines.*

**FIGURE 7C**

*This dining room includes some Feng Shui challenges. The "king and queen" chairs at either end of the table impart a feeling of inequality among the diners. The sharp corners, projecting metal legs, and invasive braces on the table are all unsafe features. The mirror tends to hurry diners along, rather than inviting them to relax and enjoy their meal.*

## A Savory View

Take a few moments to sit in each of your dining chairs, and check the view. Many people have a favorite chair with a good view and have never actually seen the views from the other chairs around their dining table. Make sure that you don't have your own version of the unpopular chair in a restaurant that has a view of the frantic, fluorescent-lit kitchen. In one case, a woman discovered that two of her dining chairs looked directly into bare light bulbs in a nearby lamp—a glaring view that she didn't have from her chair. Put all your lighting on dimmer switches so you can create the perfect dining atmosphere as needed. Also, remove eyesores such as piles of mail. Your goal is to create a place of serenity, where good digestion and stimulating conversation are assured.

### A Choice Table

**FIGURE 7D**

*The rounded corners and unobtrusive legs of this table and comfortable chairs encourage pleasant, relaxed dining.*

**FIGURE 7E**

*Put yourself in the chair to the right for a moment. The table brace will surely preoccupy you throughout the meal. The table also bares sharp corners and legs that curl out in search of unsuspecting toes and feet. The chair on the left is larger, more padded, and has more leg room than the other chair, denoting rank among diners.*

Determine if your dining table and chairs interact well together. Are you sitting too high or low to be comfortable at the table? Depending on your height and body proportions, a poor fit can occur even if you buy your dining chairs and table as a set. Can you easily scoot your chair in without hitting a brace or the base of the table? You certainly couldn't at the tables shown in Figures 7E and 7F. Most of us have hurt ourselves on dining furniture while simply trying to get seated. I remember severely bruising my knee on an ornate column that was the base for a friend's dining table—a very unpleasant experience for both of us.

**FIGURE 7F**

*Two immediate dangers—the table's sharp glass corners and large wooden base—both threaten the safety and comfort of diners.*

Likewise, choose your table shape wisely. Feng Shui favors round and oval dining tables that can be made larger or smaller according to need. This promotes flexibility, equality, and good Ch'i flow. If you prefer a rectangular table, choose one with rounded edges and corners. Glass corners, such as the one shown in Figure 7F, are considered "poison arrows" because of their dangerous sharpness.

```
┌─────────────────────────────────────────────────────┐
│                                                       │
│            CONTEMPLATIVE EXERCISE                     │
│                                                       │
│   FIND A SHARP CORNER ON A PIECE OF FURNITURE, AND SIT │
│   DIRECTLY IN FRONT OF IT. SENSE THE ENERGY COMING FROM THAT │
│   CORNER. THEN, DRAPE IT WITH FABRIC OR A VINING PLANT. SIT │
│   DIRECTLY IN FRONT OF THE CORNER AGAIN, AND SEE IF YOU SENSE A │
│   DIFFERENCE. REMEMBER, IN FENG SHUI, YOUR FEELINGS OF SAFETY │
│   AND COMFORT ARE PARAMOUNT.                          │
│                                                       │
└─────────────────────────────────────────────────────┘
```

The size of your everyday dining table is also important. A couple needs the inviting intimacy of a small table for daily use, while a family needs a larger table. When necessary, you can make large tables feel more intimate by setting one section for dining and using the rest to display beautiful flowers, fruit, sculpture, or other objects of interest. I saw this beautifully done at an Italian farmhouse. Although the family's dining table could easily accommodate 18 people, we were two of only six people dining. One end of the table was set for six, and the rest was adorned with small bronze sculptures, garlands of ivy, candles, and fresh white rose petals. The effect was stunning, and it created an intimate setting despite the table's size.

### Ceiling Fans—Calming the Atmosphere

Ceiling fans are a necessity in some climates, but when hung directly over dining tables, their blades can appear dangerously close and heavy. When a ceiling fan is too close for comfort in a dining area, it can cause people to feel irritated and argumentative and to hurry through their meals.

A family who never seemed to have a peaceful meal together had a large cherry-red fan looming directly above the dining table. The father removed it, and soon after, he reported that it was as if his family had had a personality change—for the better. His children calmed down and stopped their incessant arguing. He and his wife were able to relax and actually have a conversation with their kids and each other. Everyone spent more time at the table. The big red blades were replaced with an attractive light (on a dimmer), and a less obtrusive fan was installed nearby where it could do its job without disturbing the peace.

Hang a ceiling fan as high as possible—and not directly over furniture. A neutral-colored simple design without a light fixture is best.

### The Fine Art of Dining

Your art can positively or negatively affect the nurturing quality of your dining room. Art depicting fruits, vegetables, and flowers is appealing to most people, while dead game animals hanging by their legs is not. Landscapes, seascapes, and people enjoying a picnic are also good choices. Avoid art that is scary, unappetizing, or overpowering in color or content. If your dining room is small, use art with depth, rather than mirrors, to increase the perceived size of the room. A mirror can overactivate a dining room, especially when it is large and reflects the diners. As you may have noticed, many restaurants use bright colors, busy art, and large mirrors to hurry people through their meals.

Honor your senses at every meal by choosing the colors, textures, scents, sounds, and tastes that you want as frequent "guests" at your table. Include candles, flowers, table linens, soft music, and other enhancements that enrich your dining experience. Consider the Five Elements and the Bagua Map as you make your choices. Bring symbols of the goodness in life—the fruits of the earth—to your table. Then sit back, relax, and toast your blessings.

---

**CONTEMPLATIVE EXERCISE**

YOUR DINING ROOM REPRESENTS THE NURTURING OF YOUR BODY, HEART, AND SPIRIT. CONSIDER HOW YOU NURTURE NOT ONLY YOUR BODY, BUT YOUR EMOTIONAL NEEDS AND SPIRITUAL ASPIRATIONS AS WELL. IF YOU ARE HUNGRY ON ANY LEVEL, DECIDE HOW YOU CAN CREATE A NURTURING ATMOSPHERE THAT FEEDS THAT PARTICULAR PART OF YOU. LIFE IS A FEAST! MAKE SURE YOU'RE ENJOYING EVERY BITE.

---

**QUICK REFERENCE GUIDELINES FOR THE DINING ROOM**

- Create a tranquil atmosphere in your dining room.
- Make sure your table and chairs are safe and comfortable.
- Give each chair a pleasant view.
- Choose art that is serene and appetizing.
- Remove ceiling fans that hang directly over the dining table.
- Include enhancements that please all the senses.
- Consider the Five Elements and the Bagua Map when enhancing your dining room.

# Chapter Eight

# THE KITCHEN—
# NOURISHMENT'S BIRTHPLACE

*"Cooking is like love, it should be entered into
with abandon, or not at all."*
— Piet van Home

**FIGURE 8A**

*Friends get together for lunch in a pleasant, uncluttered kitchen. The
island provides a place to sit, as well as a good location for the stove,
where the cook can easily see the door. The fruit in the three-tiered
bowl represents the Wood element and is well placed between the stove
and the small sink, balancing the relationship between Fire and Water.*

Notice how your friends and family love to congregate in the kitchen. People are inevitably drawn to the nourishment found there. You might as well take full advantage of this natural attraction and create a kitchen that sparks your creativity—a happy, active place where you turn the bounty of food into beautiful, nourishing meals. Because the kitchen is related to the Wood element, you can easily enhance it with food from garden and orchard, such as bowls of fresh fruit, plates of nuts and baked goods, braids of garlic, pots of herbs, baskets of fresh vegetables, and vases of flowers.

It's interesting to note that, just like people, things also congregate in the kitchen—all kinds of things—from toys and shoes to homework and briefcases. Add to the mix the many gadgets we use for food preparation, and the kitchen can easily become cluttered. To keep the Ch'i flowing, and to support your desire to cook, it should be easy to return your kitchen to a clean slate after each meal.

## Countertops, not Cluttertops

**FIGURE 8B**

*The countertop in this small kitchen is too crowded to provide the cook with a clean, open surface to prepare food. This can extinguish enthusiasm and interest in cooking.*

**FIGURE 8C**

*What is used every day remains on the counter (with the exception of the knives, which were put away in a convenient drawer for safety's sake). Now the family has plenty of room to enjoy preparing the next meal.*

Take a kitchen counter survey. Along with mail and other migrating items, look for little-used appliances that clutter the area. Claim your kitchen countertops for the appliances, utensils, and food you use *on a daily basis*, and move everything else!

The motto is: "Use it every day or put it away." When you clear the decks of all the "squatters," you refresh and energize the whole kitchen, and make plenty of room for creative, enjoyable meal-making.

### Cabinets and Pantries—Behind Closed Doors

Clutter knows no boundaries. As you clear it from your countertops, inevitably you'll have to address the clutter found behind closed doors and drawers. Your kitchen pantry and cabinets can easily become over-populated with items such as empty jars, plastic containers, broken appliances, chipped dishes, and outdated or unneeded staples. Donate, recycle, or discard these things so that you have plenty of room to store the things you *do* need in your kitchen.

It is always best to store trash and recycling containers out of view. There is nothing appealing about smelling and looking at refuse when you're preparing fresh food. In most kitchens, the cabinets or pantries can be organized to accommodate trash containers so that they remain convenient, but out of sight.

Our kitchen includes six receptacles for different types of trash. Four recycling containers for paper, metal, plastic, and glass are located in the pantry closet. Our compost is collected in a covered casserole dish on the counter and emptied in the compost pile once a day. A small trash can in the cabinet beneath the sink gathers any other trash. Because our kitchen is small, each trash station takes space that had been used for other things, but once we peeled away all the kitchen clutter, there was plenty of room to store each one.

### An Eye on Safety

When you have the opportunity, design countertops that curve or undulate around the kitchen. And when the overall countertop shape is rectangular, round the corners. This helps balance the angles on kitchen appliances and equipment and gives your kitchen a safer, more inviting feeling.

Knives, although necessary tools, are sharp and can be dangerous. Make your kitchen more peaceful by storing knives and other sharp blades out of sight.

Likewise, overhead hanging racks can be hazardous. This is especially true when they are situated over places such as islands and butcher blocks, where people sit or stand. They often become cluttered with heavy items, making it difficult to get things that are "lost in space" overhead. If you need to store pots and pans in view, consider hanging them on a wall rack, where they present no threat and are easier to retrieve. Use an existing overhead rack as a decorative feature, and display a few hand-picked items as enhancements and conversation pieces.

### *The Stove—Hearth of the Kitchen*

**FIGURE 8D**

*Here, the cook has no view of what's behind her, making her feel isolated and uncomfortable. She is also impeded by clutter on the counters.*

**FIGURE 8E**

*After installing a mirror behind the stove, the cook can now see what and who is behind her. The vase of flowers to her right represents the Wood element to balance mirror (Water) and stove (Fire).*

In Feng Shui, food is associated with health and wealth. When we are prosperous, we can afford to buy the foods that build and sustain our health. If not, our ability to afford the best food is limited, and our health may suffer as a result. By buying the best, most nutritious foods we can, we sustain one of our greatest riches—good health.

Because food symbolizes a bridge between health and wealth, special attention is given to the place where food is cooked. Keep your stove clean, and use all the burners regularly, symbolizing the abundant circulation of wealth in your life.

Stoves are well placed on an island (Figure 8A), which gives the cook a commanding view, and food preparation a centralized location. If the cook's back is to the door, place a mirror, as in Figure 8E, or other reflective enhancement such as a shiny metal tray or utensil holder, behind or beside the stove. This opens up the space and provides a view of what's behind the cook.

The stove itself is related to the Fire element, while sinks and mirrors are associated with the Water element. In Five Element theory (Chapter 3), Water extinguishes Fire. If your stove is located beside your sink, or you install a mirror behind the stove, place a symbol of the Wood element nearby to activate the Nourishing Cycle of the Five Elements and balance the relationship between Water and Fire. There are many items that can symbolize Wood, including wooden spoons, bowls, and cutting boards—as well as fresh fruit, vegetables, flowers, and plants.

### Harmonious Lighting and the Kitchen Perch

Every kitchen needs a perch for visitors. If your kitchen doesn't provide space for a table and chairs, place a stool or two in a corner, or locate chairs nearby that can easily be brought in when needed. Instead of hovering in conversation, family and guests can settle in and enjoy the warmth of the kitchen.

Cooking and food preparation require good lighting, but preferably not from fluorescent lights! As energy efficient as they are, fluorescent bulbs cast a cold white light that makes people look ghostly—or perhaps ghastly. You'll make the kitchen a much more attractive place to be by replacing fluorescent lights with incandescent or halogen lighting. When this isn't possible, use full-spectrum fluorescent bulbs.

### The Bagua Map in the Kitchen

**FIGURE 8F**

*This photograph by Jan Gordon is placed in the couple's kitchen, which is in the Love and Marriage area of their home.*

Check the location of your kitchen on the Bagua Map, and if it's in an area you want to energize, be creative. When a couple discovered that their Love and Marriage area was in the kitchen, they enhanced the area with the art shown in Figure 8F. An aesthetician whose kitchen was in her Career area chose a peach fruit bowl for her kitchen counter, symbolizing "peaches 'n' cream" complexions. Use your imagination, and choose just the right kitcheny thing to enhance the Bagua area located in your kitchen.

### QUICK REFERENCE GUIDELINES FOR THE KITCHEN

- Keep your stove clean, use all burners, and give the cook a commanding view.
- Organize your countertops and cabinets.
- Choose designs that curve or have rounded corners.
- Include seating in the kitchen.
- Replace or minimize the use of fluorescent lighting.
- Include the Five Elements, and enhance the kitchen according to the Bagua Map.

# Chapter Nine

# THE FAMILY ROOM—
# YOUR INDOOR PLAYGROUND

*"Playing is a basic animal instinct. We are at
our most appealing when at play."*
— Ilse Crawford

The family room is often the most versatile room in the house. As a room meant for play and relaxation, it functions best when everyone's needs are addressed. The magical family room must be able to "change hats" quickly to be a child's romper room, a teenager's lounge, a dining area, an exercise studio, a dance hall, and a home movie theater. To achieve this, family members need space to express themselves, as well as easy-to-use storage space.

When a family room lacks storage, chaos reigns. Adults and children alike will put their stuff away much faster when they can put it away *in the same room* without having to cart it somewhere else. The easier it is to get things out and to put them away, the more likely it is that order will have the upper hand. Give each family member a chest, trunk, drawer, or cabinet, such as the one in Figure 9A, where they can quickly and easily stash their belongings.

**FIGURE 9A**

*Family rooms need areas to display books and other treasures, as well as storage for every member of the family.*

**FIGURE 9B**

*Electrical equipment such as televisions are best housed in cabinets with doors.*

Clients with two daughters, ages six and nine, had a family room that looked like the aftermath of a hurricane in a toy store. Everything, including the television and the girls' many toys, were out all the time, making it a permanently chaotic romper room. The parents did three things. First, they gave each child a large, lightweight wicker "treasure chest" where they could store their toys between romps. The chests fit side by side against a wall where the kids could easily get to them. Second, they cleaned out a nearby closet for the girls' larger toys. (This started what I call the Feng Shui domino effect. Clean out one closet, and before you know it, all the closets are knocked open for inspection and clearance.) And third, they bought a cabinet with doors for their television. With places to store toys and other things when not in use, the family room became "fun-ctional" for everyone, enhancing harmony in the family, and increasing the happy, healthy energy flowing through the house.

### Protecting Your Natural Rhythms

Many Feng Shui practitioners consider electrical equipment an enhancement. And *it is,* when properly used, well taken care of, and appreciated by the owners. Most family rooms are full of electrical equipment, including computers, stereos, and televisions. They can be a fabulous source of information and entertainment; or they can devour family time, romantic interludes, and peaceful solitude.

Conceal your equipment in built-in cabinets (Figure 9B) or in ready-made furniture with doors. Or cover equipment with fitted cloths or fabric that suits the decor of the room. Our credo for balance is "Out of sight, out of mind." Usually when a TV is visible all the time, it's also on, turning a wonderful helpmate into an unfortunate master. Dedicate your family room to your family's natural rhythms, which are served *occasionally* by your television and other such equipment.

### Family Furnishings

Choose no-nonsense family room furniture that can be bumped, spilled on, and otherwise abused without damage. A round or oval distressed wood table, with several leaves to make it larger for special occasions, is an example of a good family room table. Make this room friendly and supportive by using very durable, comfortable fabrics, floor coverings, and furniture. The Ch'i of family happiness flows best when your family room is as indestructible as possible. Use the same guidelines found in the Living Room chapter (page 105) to arrange your family room furniture.

## *Happy Enhancements*

The family room is the place for bright, happy art and colors. A rogue's gallery of family photos, children's art, bulletin boards posted with the latest family events, whimsical collections of toys and games, and anything that's playful and fun are great in the family room. Locate your family room on the Bagua Map (Chapter 2), and choose art, colors, and other appointments that correlate with it. It's also a good place for bookshelves, with a comfortable place to read and ample reading light nearby.

---

### CONTEMPLATIVE EXERCISE

CONTEMPLATE THE RELATIONSHIPS YOU HAVE WITH YOUR FAMILY AND FRIENDS. DETERMINE WHETHER EACH RELATIONSHIP IS HOW YOU'D LIKE IT TO BE. IF IT'S NOT LOVING AND SUPPORTIVE, DECIDE WHAT YOU CAN DO TO IMPROVE IT. THINK ABOUT WHAT YOU HAVE LEARNED AND WHAT "HIDDEN GIFTS" YOU'VE RECEIVED FROM THIS RELATIONSHIP. IT MAY HAVE HELPED YOU LEARN TO SET BOUNDARIES, OVERCOME CHALLENGES, OR BE STRONG IN THE FACE OF OPPOSITION. WHEN YOU CULTIVATE FORGIVENESS AND LET GO OF THE PAST, YOU ARE FREE TO ATTRACT AND ENJOY LOVING RELATIONSHIPS NOW.

---

**QUICK REFERENCE GUIDELINES FOR THE FAMILY ROOM**

- Provide plenty of storage for each family member's belongings.
- Put electronic equipment behind closed doors.
- Furnish with indestructibility and comfort in mind.
- Refer to the suggestions for living rooms, Chapter 6, page 105.
- Include joyful, happy art—and shelves for family books.
- Take the Bagua Map and the Five Elements into consideration.

# Chapter Ten

# THE HOME OFFICE—
# A POWERHOUSE
# OF PRODUCTIVITY

*"An office environment can nourish and support the
human spirit as much as it can deny and suppress it.
If our offices are humane, loving, and sacred, then what
is produced in those offices will have a sense of humanity
and integrity. . . . The act of turning the places where we
work into places that we love, can transform our
own lives, and will in turn positively affect the
lives of everyone around us."*
— Denise Linn

Make your home office your place of power. What you do there leads directly to your prosperity and success. Whether your work is action-packed or introspective, full- or part-time, your home office needs to be specifically organized and arranged to enhance your discipline, creativity, and success.

**FIGURE 10A**

*This was the home office of a marketing consultant before improvements. His back was to the door, and the room was very disorganized. The Fire element, seen in the red chair, fiery rug, and large tiger painting, dominated the room. This correlated with the man's ongoing problems involving volatile and unpleasant clients. (**Also in color, page 120.**)*

**FIGURE 10B**

*Improvements included repositioning the desk to command the room and provide a view of the door. The desk's frosted glass, black supports, black computer mat, and crystal bowl represent the cooling influence of the Water element. The fiery rug was removed to correct the overabundance of the Fire element and improve movement of the desk chair. Filing and other organizational systems were designed to match the man's style and keep him organized. Soon after these changes were made, he was given an ongoing full-time project by his favorite client. (**Also in color, page 120.**)*

### *Locating Your Office Within Your Home*

The more active and people-oriented your work, the more you will benefit from an office in the front of the house. Up-front locations work especially well when you or others come and go frequently, such as in many sales or product-based vocations.

When your work is more contemplative and inwardly focused, your ideal work location is toward the back of the house. Back bedrooms and dens usually provide the atmosphere necessary for artists, writers, and anyone needing peace and quiet to work.

**Desk Placement:** No matter where your home office is located, take the reins of success in hand by arranging the room to serve you in every detail. Of primary importance is the placement of your desk. The desk's ideal power position is where you have a perfect view of the door from your chair, a pleasant view out a window, and a solid wall behind you (Figure 10B). This gives you complete support from the back and a commanding view from the front. Notice how top executives never sit with their backs to the door. If there is more than one power place in the room, sit in each spot for a few minutes to determine which you like best. Most people are more comfortable located to one side of the door or the other—not directly in front of it. This affords a sense of added protection, while maintaining a commanding view.

Claiming the power position in your home office often means positioning your desk or work table like an island in the room, rather than pushing it against a wall—so your desk should be attractive from all angles, without exposed nests of wires or unfinished sides. Enclose wires in a tube designed to hold them (available at any office supply store) and run them safely out of harm's way under area rugs or existing carpeting. When possible, design your home office space with electrical outlets in the middle of the floor so that you won't have to run wires over to a wall.

You can also buy a desk designed with an opening behind a front panel where wires remain out of sight and the front of the desk "shows well." Unsightly desk panels can be transformed with a new coat of stain or paint, or hidden behind short screens, plants, book shelves, or furniture. Desks can also be slipcovered, with attractive fabric fitted over the top and around three sides. Add a piece of glass that covers the fabric on the desktop, and you have a brand new desk.

**FIGURE 10C**

*The desk in this health profession-al's home office was built in with no view of the door.*

**FIGURE 10D**

*The mirror gives her a perfect view of the door, relax-ing her nervous system and empowering her work. When the mirror was first installed, the reflection doubled the clutter, moti-vating her to clean and clear her home office.*

### *Making the Very Best of Your Location*

While it's ideal to have a view of both door and window in your home office, a view of the door is more important. If you lose a good window view in order to see the door, hang a mirror to reflect the view while you're at your desk. If a window is located directly behind your desk, enhance your sense of stability and protection by placing something substantial—such as a large plant or credenza—between you and the window. If you cannot bear to give up your window view, install a mirror so that you can see the door from your desk.

Because mirrors enlarge and brighten a room, they activate energy and are well placed in a home office. As shown in Figure 10D, a strategically placed mirror can also improve a room when you can't move your office furniture to gain a view of the door. Use a free-standing or wall-mounted mirror so that it reflects the door behind you when you are seated at your desk. Small compact or shaving mirrors also work well, since their purpose is not necessarily to reflect *you*, but any motion occurring behind you. Art with reflective glass can also be used to catch any movement behind you.

Ideally, mirrors reflect harmonious images, so make sure that the reflection isn't doubling unpleasant views. Improve the room by uncluttering the space and adding items such as flowers, art, and attractive window treatments.

### *Furnishing Your Home Office*

There are several guidelines to keep in mind as you are furnishing your home office. First, as with all rooms, keep stress and irritability to a minimum by choosing furniture with rounded corners, or positioning things with sharp corners out of the traffic flow. You can also turn furniture with sharp corners like filing cabinets at a diagonal in the room (as in Figure 10B), or store them in closets.

Second, when choosing your desk or work table(s), decide what size and design will suit you best. You may need more than one working surface in the room to accommodate your needs, so determine what height interacts well with your chair. Also, figure out where your office equipment, such as computer, fax machine, and printer should be placed; and what other furniture—reading chair, conference table, bookshelves—are needed in the room.

I have discovered that I work best at a large round table with several chairs around it, much like a dining room table. Each chair is a "station" where I place specific work. Throughout the day, I move from chair to chair, working on various projects. I enjoy getting up and moving around the table, and I can easily move work from station to station as the project progresses. A mirror reflects the door from the station that has no view. This unique style has evolved out of my observations on what works for me, rather than my adapting to what office furniture stores have to offer. In your home office, you are creating your personal powerhouse of productivity, efficiency, and creativity. Meet all your needs as closely as possible.

Third, rectangular, circular, oval, or kidney-shaped desks or work surfaces are best. Whenever you have a work area that faces away from the door, install a mirror or art framed in reflective glass to reflect the door. The ideal shapes for conference tables are circular or oval, as they sustain an active flow of harmony and equality around the table.

Fourth, although your desk's color and material are personal choices, most people work best at a surface where white paper contrasts just right. Paper tends to disappear on pure white surfaces and contrast dramatically on black surfaces. Either extreme can cause eyestrain. Clear glass desks seem to disappear beneath paper, which can also strain the eyes. Most wooden or medium-toned surfaces provide the right amount of contrast without visual strain.

And fifth, your desk chair is your throne. Consider it a vital piece of office equipment, and choose the most comfortable seat possible. This cannot be emphasized enough. Your capacity to produce and prosper is considerably enhanced by a great work chair. Treat yourself to an ergonomically correct chair that has excellent lumbar support and adjustable height. Most people thrive in one that rocks back and forth, has five legs, sturdy casters, a high back, a headrest, and adjustable armrests. Always sit in a chair before you buy it—that's the only way to know if you've truly found your throne.

### *Electromagnetic Fields*

The electromagnetic field (EMF) of electrical and battery-powered equipment is also a concern in your home office. You probably sit at least six feet away from a television, but what about all the other electrical equipment you use? An electromagnetic field tester will give you an idea of what EMF you are exposed to when you use your computer, fax machine, and phone, as well as your hair dryer, shaver, microwave, and blender. You'd be surprised by how much EMF you are bathed in each day. One client now uses a headset to avoid the high electromagnetic field around his cordless phone, while another moved her fax machine away from her desk. Your best defense is to know what level of EMF your appliances and equipment generate, and then to use them less or stay out of their field of radiation, usually a minimum of three feet.

### *Getting and Staying Organized*

Being organized in your home office is not an option—it's mandatory. Powerful, productive Ch'i cannot find its way through clutter or chaos. Become the "samurai of clutter," and slice through any tendency to pile up extraneous catalogs, magazines, newsletters, and papers in the corners and around the edges of your office. This is crucial to your creativity, energy level, and ability to attract new opportunities. I have seen many home offices that doubled as chaotic storerooms or were piled with years' worth of junk mail and papers. In every case, the chaos had ground productivity to a halt. To be effective, your office needs to be returned to order on a regular basis so that the newest projects and creative endeavors have a place to flourish.

If you find yourself hip-deep in chaos and can't seem to pull yourself out, don't despair! Hire a professional organizer to identify your personal work style and help you organize your work space accordingly. With or without the help of such a person in your life, it's critical to discover your personal work style so that you can maintain an organized and clutter-free home office. For instance, you may be a person like me who needs piles, not files, to work effectively.

From my perspective, files are where papers disappear forever. I have to see my projects while I'm working on them. To keep myself organized, I have a wall of floor-to-ceiling shelves that are 24 inches deep. Their generous depth provides room for papers I need to see. Behind them, there's plenty of room for my reference books and teaching manuals. Once I'm done with a project, I can file it away, but not until then. Before I installed my wall of shelves, I had piles of work and books arranged like a "floor-al" wreath around my desk. The shelves provide a far more organized and pleasing way for me to see what I'm working on.

### Office Sensuality

To personalize your home office, turn to your five senses. Remember, your office is your worldly battery where you plug in and produce! You probably aren't going to be "juiced" by looking at leftover art, mismatched furniture, or drab colors all day. Give each of your senses serious consideration. Decide what sights, sounds, tastes, smells, and feelings elicit power, creativity, energy, and resourcefulness in you.

One client chose a rosewood desk and paintings of wild horses as visual enhancements. He draws inspiration from Vivaldi and other classical music, drinks French roast coffee in fine china, and loves his big leather chair. Another client wouldn't dream of such an office. She works in the ethereal glow of Gilbert Williams prints, lavender walls, and plenty of natural light. Her music is by New Age artists such as Yanni and Raphael, she drinks spring water from a crystal decanter, and rocks in a deep purple ergonomically correct chair. Her husband's home office is "clothed" in the natural look of oak furniture, golden walls, and framed posters of beautiful scenery. He drinks his green tea from an earthenware mug, sits in a high-backed office chair, and listens to the gurgling sound of a small desktop waterfall.

Surround yourself with the things that keep you inspired, creative, and productive. Your home office is the place where you manifest great things in the world. Make it your powerhouse. You'll be richly rewarded when you do.

### Power Bagua—Mapping Office and Desk

Use the Bagua Map (Chapter 2) to power up your office. With your Bagua Map in hand, stand at your office door and face the room. From this vantage point, determine which area of the Map you are entering the room through, usually Knowledge and Self-Cultivation, Career, or Helpful People and Travel. For instance, in Figure 10B, the entrance into the room is through Helpful People and Travel. The large tiger print behind the desk is in the Fame and Reputation area, symbolizing power and focus in business. The fax machine is located in the Love and Marriage area, enhancing communications between consultant and clients. The Wealth and Prosperity area is enhanced with printer and banking files, and the shelves in the Health and Family area hold personal papers and files. The consultant systematically enhanced every Bagua area in his home office, bringing tremendous Ch'i and success into his business. You can do the same, giving special attention to the areas that correlate with your current goals in life. Placing objects in your home office that anchor the various Bagua areas stimulate and sustain your creative juices, and provide your office with inner meaning as well as outer warmth and balance.

**FIGURE 10E**

*Here is one example of a desk arranged according to the Bagua Map. The computer is in the Career area; reference books in Knowledge and Self-Cultivation; floral boxes holding a "family" of office supplies in Health and Family; a crystal bowl and calculator in Wealth and Prosperity; a lamp in Fame and Reputation; a photo and a vase with two roses in Love and Marriage; pens and markers in Children and Creativity; and a telephone in Helpful People and Travel.*

The Bagua Map can also increase the flow of Ch'i around your desk. Your "entrance," as seen in Figure 10E, is where you sit at the desk, usually in the Career area. From your seat, determine where each Gua is located on the desk. Straight ahead, at the back center of your desk, is the Fame and Reputation area. This is a perfect place on your desk to display things that stir your sense of accomplishment and represent your good reputation, such as awards and certificates you've earned. And because Fame and Reputation is associated with the element of Fire, you can also choose things that represent Fire, such as a lamp, photos of animals or people, or red items such as flowers, frames, or supply holders. The more personally empowering your selections are, the more they build and sustain your productivity and success. Map your desk, and as with your room, pay special attention to enhancing the Guas that correlate with the areas in your life you'd like to improve.

## QUICK REFERENCE GUIDELINES FOR THE HOME OFFICE

- Choose a location in the home that suits your vocation.
- Place yourself in the power position of your office.
- After determining your needs, choose safe, comfortable, pleasing furniture.
- Maintain an organized, clutter-free space.
- Empower all your senses.
- Enhance your office and your desk according to the Bagua Map.

# Chapter Eleven

# BEDROOMS—
# SENSUAL SERENITY

*"The bedroom is shaped by the peace of sleep, the flights
of dream, and the charged energies of sexuality...the
bedroom contains unfathomable mysteries and power."*
— Anthony Lawlor

Serenity and sensuality—two prerequisites for a healthy, happy existence—are often missing in our Western culture, and the bedroom is
where we can find them. Bedrooms are meant for sleeping, reading,
reflecting, romancing, and recharging your batteries—a perfect antidote
for a busy, stressful day. Because every part of your life is connected, the
quality of rest you receive in your bedroom is crucial to your happiness,
health, and productivity. A cozy, sensual bedroom atmosphere invites
complete rest and rejuvenation of your body, mind, and spirit.

Unfortunately, there are many bedrooms that don't function well as
places of rest. While other rooms in the house are nicely appointed, the
bedroom may be drearily furnished in old college leftovers accented with
clashing linens and unframed poster art. The thought is that the bedroom
isn't important because "nobody sees it," and we "don't spend much time
there, anyway." Well, no wonder! When asked, many people admit that
they don't sleep well and are chronically exhausted. And romantic interests? They're just too tired to pursue them.

Feng Shui presents a new perspective. Bedrooms are related to the Metal element, connoting the act of "digging in" under soft, earthy covers and being embraced in quiet comfort. But bedrooms treated like forgotten stepchildren cannot nurture and rejuvenate you. When you make it a priority to bring serenity and sensuality into your bedroom, the room you may have spent years avoiding becomes an inviting sanctuary. Each night, you are drawn like a magnet to its welcoming embrace, where you sleep well, are deeply refreshed, and are reenergized for the day's activities.

**FIGURE 11A**

*This bedroom includes warm colors, soft linens, favorite art, and an overall simple and serene design.* ***(Also in color, page 121.)***

I consider my bedroom a sacred retreat. My husband, Brian, and I relish its quiet atmosphere, where we fall into the bed's friendly embrace after long and active days. It is a serene, inviting, and uncomplicated room. There is a king-sized bed, two reading lamps, two nightstands, and a small table for candles. Our bed is dressed in heaps of down comforters and pillows covered in gold and deep red flannel. A Chinese screen carved with a nocturnal scene makes up our headboard. Art includes a large burnished gold fan painted with nesting cranes, and a Balinese angel. The floor is covered with handwoven carpets in deep shades of red, blue, and gold. There is no television, and, except when there's a family concern, the telephone ringer is turned off. Curtains open to a view of the back garden, and they close to turn the room blissfully dark, even in the middle of the day. There, enfolded in sensual warmth and serenity, we find a place for rest, romance, and rejuvenation.

### *Furnishings and Decor—Designing the Perfect Nest*

The comfort and safety you feel in the world is directly connected to how safe and comfortable you feel in your home. Obviously, bedrooms should be especially so. Choose art for over the bed that is either lightweight, such as textiles and swags (Figure 11B), or that is solidly anchored to the wall. Don't place heavy, loose objects such as the metal stars shown in Figure 11C over your bed. When it comes to furnishings, choose styles without sharp corners or edges that could be dangerous to sleepy—or amorous—body parts. Avoid protruding metal legs, pointed objects, or sharp detailing that can do serious damage, as shown in Figures 11D and 11E. Choose designs and materials that won't send you to the hospital because of one wrong move.

**FIGURE 11B**

*Even if this artful swag of ribbons and raffia fell, there'd be no harm done. Made by its owner, it symbolizes the union between her and her husband. Nightstands and lamps on both sides of the bed symbolize equality in their relationship.*

**FIGURE 11C**

*Solid metal stars dangle precariously over a youngster's bed. This is not the place for heavy art that's poorly installed. When you want to hang something heavy over the bed, secure it well so that there's no chance it could fall.*

**FIGURE 11D**

*At first glance, this bedroom looks inviting, but there is a big Feng Shui problem with the design of the bed frame.*

**FIGURE 11E**

*The metal detailing on the bed frame is knife-edge sharp and could tear fabric or hurt someone.*

Mirrors activate energy in the bedroom and can interfere with a good night's sleep by causing restlessness and insomnia. The bigger a mirror is, and the closer it is to the bed, the more likely it is to disturb your sleep. Because many bedrooms in Western homes double as dressing rooms, it's often impractical to remove mirrors such as mirrored closet doors. In this case, you can have the best of both worlds by draping them like a window, as shown in Figures 4N and 4O on page 83. Then, you "open up" the mirror during the day, and "close" it at night.

### Memories and Associations—"Who" Are You Sleeping with Tonight?

Because your possessions are essentially alive, it's very important that your connection with every object in your bedroom elicits a positive, nurturing response. Does anything carry unpleasant memories? Don't allow your possessions to engulf you with negative feelings, thoughts, or associations, especially in the bedroom, where daily first and last impressions are made.

One client had bought her gorgeous bedroom furniture with her ex-husband decades ago, and hadn't had one date in the six years since her divorce. When she looked through Feng Shui eyes, her very expensive furniture became quite expressive. Suddenly she could hear the "chatter" of memories and associations concerning her marriage, his infidelity, and their divorce court drama. Did she want these memories kept alive in her daily life? No! She wanted to move forward, not backward. She decided to let go of furniture that chained her to the past and purchase a suite that represented new beginnings. Her comment was, "No wonder I couldn't put my divorce to *bed*!"

---

**CONTEMPLATIVE EXERCISE**

ASK YOURSELF WHAT MEMORIES, THOUGHTS, FEELINGS, AND ASSOCIATIONS LIVE IN YOUR BEDROOM. WHAT IS EACH ITEM "SAYING" EACH TIME YOU LOOK AT IT? CLEANSE YOUR BEDROOM OF ITEMS THAT KEEP NEGATIVE MEMORIES AND ASSOCIATIONS ALIVE, AND YOU'LL FIND THAT YOUR BEDROOM WILL EMBRACE AND REVITALIZE YOU.

---

**FIGURE 11F**

*Exercise equipment can be very "talkative," especially when you don't use it as often as you think you should. It's best to move your exercise equipment to another room or screen it from the bed.*

**FIGURE 11G**

*Because there is no other place in the house for the exercise bike, the owner uses a lightweight screen that can easily be moved as needed.*

### Desks, Exercise Equipment, and Other Strange Bedfellows

Along with things that carry unwanted associations and memories, there are other items you may not want to have in your bedroom. Desks and exercise equipment are associated with activity and can chase the feeling of serenity right out of the room. Desks are "awake" with work, bills, and unfinished business that require action, while Nordic tracks or stationary bikes are constantly reminding you to get up and exercise. Just when you need to rest, these two "action figures" pipe up and announce that a report is due or that you're looking a little flabby. Conversely, when you see the bed from the desk or bike, it can suggest nap time.

I noticed this when I lived in a studio apartment. Because I could see my bed from my desk, and vice versa, I would lie in bed thinking about how much work I had to do, and feel sleepy sitting at my desk. I solved the problem and improved the view with a six-panel wooden screen that defined two distinct areas—an awake place where I could work well, and a place dedicated to rest.

To maintain peace and tranquillity in the bedroom, dedicate it to its original role—the room for the *bed*. Make the bed the ruler, and locate possessions that require activity somewhere else. When you have no other option, move "active" furniture and equipment as far away from the bed as possible (Figures 11F and 11G), and cover or screen them so that you don't see them from the bed. Furniture that suggests relaxation, such as chaise lounges and reading chairs, make nice additions to a bedroom's atmosphere.

### The View from the Bed—First and Last Impressions

In Feng Shui, your bed is ideally located where you have a view of the door, without being directly in front of it. This puts you in an "eddy" of the room, while maintaining a view of the door. When your bed has to be directly in front of the door, place a substantial foot board, trunk, or other piece of furniture at the foot of the bed to suggest protection between you and the door. Or, curtain or canopy the bed to screen it from the door, making sure that you can see enough of the door through the curtain to feel comfortable. Likewise, if a window is directly over the head of your bed, include a substantial headboard and window treatments to remove you from direct exposure and promote the feeling of

**FIGURE 11H**

*Here, there is no separation between bedroom and bath. This leaves the bathroom lacking in privacy and the bedroom lacking in tranquillity.*

**FIGURE 11I**

*A palm tree and a shoji screen that matches the closet doors improve both the view and the sense of privacy and tranquillity, while maintaining easy access to the bathroom.*

safety. Your bed can also be placed at a diagonal in the room when you have a solid headboard or screen behind you.

Your view from the bed influences your view of the world. Make it a good one! Improve a view that takes you straight into a chaotic closet or bathroom, such as the one shown in Figure 11H, and replace art that isn't either sensual or serene. Making a structural change such as moving or adding a door may not be possible, but in almost every case, you can shut, curtain, or screen open passageways, as shown in Figures 11H and 11I. Create a tranquil view with art, healthy plants, restful colors, or a calming arrangement of items. Choose objects or elements you find pleasing, knowing that this is what you see first thing in the morning and last thing at night.

### Closets and Bureaus—Pockets of Plenty

You are just as connected to what's behind closed doors and drawers as you are to anything else in your home. Because the flow of possessions is so abundant in our Western culture, bedroom closets and bureaus are easily overwhelmed with excess garments and accessories, restricting the harmonious flow of Ch'i through your bedroom and your life. Take an honest look into your "pockets of plenty" on a regular basis, and rid them of excess weight. Figures 11J and 11K show a client's closet before and after she cleaned and organized it. She was amazed at what a difference it made in her mental clarity and emotional well-being. Don't underestimate the importance of doing this. In Feng Shui, private chaos is just as depleting as public chaos. It all counts. Many bedrooms appear to be neat until you open a closet door, and then all clutter breaks loose. What you see every day in the privacy of your own "drawers" is making a continual impression on you. It's vital that you make that impression a good one.

**FIGURE 11J**

*A jumbled, chaotic closet promotes confusion, a sense of being overwhelmed, and a lack of personal power.*

**FIGURE 11K**

*An orderly closet promotes clarity, peacefulness, and personal power. When you want to attract positive opportunities and experiences, clean out a closet. It works every time.*

One of my greatest personal discoveries is this: When I let go of something that I don't need, what I *do* need manifests in my life. By clearing out the old, I make room for the new, and the quality of my life continues to get better and better. I first discovered this when, as a Feng Shui practitioner, I was "forced" to attend to my closet. God forbid anyone see it in the chaotic shape it was in. It was like a garden that hadn't been weeded in years. Confusion reigned, and every day I had to fight through the jumble just to get dressed. I decided to follow the lead of a friend who, along with being exceptionally successful in life, had her closet arranged by color. All the white pants were grouped together, followed by those in yellow, red, blue, purple, brown, and black. Same with the shirts and dresses. Her closet always looked like a rainbow.

As I moved items around and sorted out the excess, I assembled a large pile of giveaways. With them out of the way, I could see what I owned as well as what I needed. This gave me an idea. I called a dozen women friends and asked them to weed their closets for items to bring to a clothing exchange. What we didn't claim by the end of the night could go to the local women's shelter. Two weeks later we were all running around in our underwear trying on each other's clothes. Our one rule: Take only what you need. No hoarding! Each of us walked away with new treasures and great memories, while the shelter received ten bags of clothes, shoes, and accessories. Since then, our clothing exchange has become a yearly tradition.

Set aside the time to look through your closets, bureaus, and jewelry boxes, and gather items that you no longer use or want. Then pass them on by selling or giving them away, and make a note of when you did so. For the next 30 days, see what opportunities, synchronistic experiences, and new possessions flow into your life that you really do need and want.

### Sense Appeal

Because we honor the five senses in the practice of Feng Shui, we focus on creating truly sensual environments. Whether single or coupled, your bedroom should be a place where all your senses are comforted and intimately celebrated. Here you can light a scented candle, play bedroom music, and relax. This is your oasis in which to have treats that you enjoy—anything from tea and croissants to champagne and strawberries.

Here is the place to splurge on fabrics that are sensual, including chenille, flannel, silk, cotton, satin, and velvet.

The best bedroom colors are found in the skin tones of all the races—pearly beiges and tans, creamy cocoas, blushing pinks and peaches, subtle yellows, pale violets, and earthy reds. There is a wide variety of warm pastel colors, as well as more pigmented rich tones such as coral, chocolate, butter cream, terra-cotta, cinnabar, raspberry, aubergine, burgundy, copper, gold, and bronze. Pure white, gray, black, blues, and gray greens can create a gorgeous look, but when they dominate, they make the room too chilly to be sensual.

In one case, a young couple had chosen a contemporary black lacquer bedroom suite, and they set it against gray walls and carpet. Beneath their black duvet were dark green and steel-gray sheets. Their intention to create a "cool" bedroom succeeded quite literally. They complained of a general lack of libido and a life that included very little fun.

To balance their bedroom, they bought linens, area rugs, and other accents in vanilla and raspberry to complement their existing furniture. They also painted the walls a rich vanilla and added several nude paintings in complementary skin tones. The result was a delicious visual treat. Their "ice palace" thawed and became a welcoming place in which to unwind and enjoy each other. In fact, they often go to bed now for "dessert."

If your bedroom is decorated in cool colors, bring in complementary warm tones. This can be done in many ways—a new coat of paint, sheets, pillowcases, pillows, throws, art, comforters, slipcovers, rugs, tablecloths, flowers, and candles. And, as always, be sure your choice turns you on!

---

### CONTEMPLATIVE EXERCISE

WHAT ARE SOME OF THE MOST ENJOYABLE WAYS TO SOOTHE YOUR SENSES OF SIGHT, HEARING, SMELL, TOUCH, AND TASTE? MAKE A LIST OF WHAT ENGAGES AND DELIGHTS EACH SENSE, AND ADD TO IT AS YOU THINK OF NEW IDEAS. IF YOU SHARE A BEDROOM, ASK YOUR PARTNER WHAT HE OR SHE IS SENSUALLY NURTURED BY, AND INCORPORATE THOSE IDEAS AS WELL. YOU SHOULD BE STRUCK WITH THE SENSUAL QUALITIES OF YOUR BEDROOM EVERY MORNING AND NIGHT.

---

### *Artful Embrace*

The art in your bedroom makes a strong impact on your psyche. Make it a positive one! Include sensual, serene, or romantic images that calm and inspire you. Exclude three-ring circuses, busy cityscapes, action figures, or art depicting unhappy or gruesome subjects.

A woman who suffered from insomnia brought on by "performance anxiety" at work had a three-ring circus in full performance over her bed. Not only was the painting extremely busy, but it was also very large and heavy. To complement it, she'd added a wallpaper border of prancing circus animals that marched around the room. She'd chosen the art and borders because they matched the teal and terra-cotta color scheme of her bedroom. It had never occurred to her that the content and placement of her art might be rubbing her nervous system the wrong way. She moved the circus to the family room and noticed herself calming down immediately. Several weeks later, her work assignment was changed to one that was much less stressful and more enjoyable for her.

### *The Television in the Bedroom—Who's Watching Whom?*

I visit many clients who enjoy watching television in their bedrooms. When this is the case, I strongly suggest that they store the TV in an armoire or cabinet such as the one in Figures 11L and 11M. Televisions can be very compelling and tend to get the lion's share of attention when visible in the room. Most television programming consists of either action stories or bad news, neither of which is conducive to deep, restorative sleep. What we need before sleep is introspection, inspiration, and tranquillity. Before retiring at night, consider writing in your journal, reading, or reflecting on your day, rather than watching television.

**FIGURE 11L**

*Bedroom televisions are best placed inside a cabinet or armoire . . .*

**FIGURE 11M**

*. . . so that they can be "put to bed" between uses. Notice how much calmer the bedroom appears when the armoire doors are closed. This room also features stenciling by artist Jacki Powell that draws the line between heaven and earth, and balances the vaulted ceiling.*

**FIGURE 11N**

*This woman is sleeping with her head to the north, the direction that strengthens her physical health and vitality.*

### Directional Sleeping

People of all ages can benefit from sleeping with their *heads* facing north, south, east, or west, depending on their needs at the time. In general, when your head is pointing north, like the woman in Figure 11N, your health and vitality are strengthened. This is often the best direction for us to sleep. But let's consider the benefits of the other directions. Heading south enhances intuition and can stimulate dream and memory recall. Heading west tends to slow life down and is helpful when the stress of life causes restlessness or insomnia; heading east tends to speed life up, lifting sluggishness and depression. Sleeping northwest, northeast, southwest, or southeast blends the qualities of the two directions. For instance, directing the head northwest helps to strengthen physical health and slow life down, while sleeping with the head southeast stimulates intuition and dream recall and increases energy.

One mother discovered that her hyperactive son slept with his head directed to the east. She put his pillow at the other end of the bed so that his head pointed west, and he calmed down dramatically "overnight." Conversely, another mom turned the head of her teenage son's bed to the east because he was impossible to rouse in the morning, and from then on he never missed the school bus again.

---

**CONTEMPLATIVE EXERCISE**

YOUR BEDROOM IS YOUR PLACE TO DIVE DEEP—INTO DREAMING AND DREAMINESS; INTO LOVEMAKING; AND INTO THE RENEWAL OF BODY, MIND, AND SPIRIT. TAKE A FEW MINUTES AND REFLECT ON YOUR FEELINGS ABOUT BEDROOMS. BEGIN WITH YOUR FIRST BEDROOM MEMORIES AND THE FEELINGS ASSOCIATED WITH THOSE MEMORIES. THEN ONE BY ONE, REMEMBER ALL THE BEDROOMS THROUGHOUT YOUR LIFE. WRITE DOWN WHAT YOU LIKED AND DISLIKED ABOUT EACH ONE, SUCH AS THE SIZE, THE PLAY OF LIGHT, THE COLORS, THE WAY THE BED WAS PLACED, THE LINENS, THE CLOSETS, THE DOORS, THE FURNITURE, AND THE ART. ALSO, TAKE NOTE OF THE FEELINGS ASSOCIATED WITH EACH ROOM. TAKE THE WARMEST AND MOST POSITIVE MEMORIES AND FEELINGS ON YOUR LIST AND BRING THEM INTO THE DESIGN OF YOUR CURRENT BEDROOM. IF YOU SHARE THE BEDROOM WITH A PARTNER, ASK HIM OR HER TO DO THE SAME THING, AND INCLUDE THOSE IDEAS AS WELL.

---

**Please note:** *You can do this exercise with respect to any room in the house.*

## Master Bedrooms

I have the opportunity to work with many couples, and I often notice how accurately their master bedroom reflects their relationship. Fifty percent of American marriages end in divorce, and now that I've seen a vast sampling of master bedrooms, I can see why. New couples optimistically assume that the strength of their relationship will last a lifetime. But through the daily grind of Western life, they often notice a decline in their libido. Many couples don't realize that an environment can strengthen and nourish, or dampen and weaken, their intimacy. They often place little importance on their bedroom environment, assuming that it doesn't affect their relationship. But, like water dripping on a stone, their bedrooms make an impression, little by little, night after day, for better or for worse, through sickness and through health, until death—or divorce—do them part. The more active and "crazy" a couple's lifestyle is, the more crucial it is that they have a private and appealing bedroom sanctuary in which to rest, rejuvenate, and connect with one another.

**Encouraging Intimacy:** There are many ways in which couples can encourage intimacy. Books and magazine articles provide countless suggestions on finding and keeping a loving relationship. Feng Shui adds a unique vantage point by addressing the subtle (and not-so-subtle) aspects of arranging the master bedroom. Along with the suggestions on bedrooms in the previous pages, couples can nurture and enhance intimacy by thoughtfully sewing some very special threads into the fabric of their bedrooms.

A newly married couple was given the wedding gift of a Feng Shui consultation. I found that their master bedroom had many challenges. The wife's side of the bed had an open view into the bathroom's toilet and sink. The husband's side was crowded with the laundry hamper and an exercise bicycle. Neither side had a nightstand or lamp. The entire room was white, accented with denim blue linens. Light streamed in (and Ch'i streamed out) through large, undraped windows. There was no coziness or sensuality to be found.

I recommended many of the ideas presented in this chapter: Paint the walls a warm, inviting color; choose linens in delicious colors and sensuous textures; screen or curtain the bathroom door; purchase nightstands and lamps; treat the windows; add bedroom art; and relocate the bike and the laundry basket. These were the top priorities for turning their master bedroom into an intimate, relaxing place. To further cultivate the room's sensual personality, I suggested that they light candles and listen to soft music. It was at this point in our conversation that the wife exclaimed, "Now I know what's happened to our sex life!"

**Bigger Is Not Always Better:** In Feng Shui, there's a saying that the bigger the master bedroom, the higher the divorce rate. This stems from the fact that it's often challenging to make a large multi-use master suite into a cozy, intimate nest. Feng Shui observes that we are most comfortable in an environment that is neither too big (Yang) nor too small (Yin). Large Yang bedrooms need Yin features such as rich textured fabrics, canopies, area rugs and drapes, as well as small, cozy areas defined within the suite. This may include a canopied bed in one area—especially effective when the bedroom ceiling is high—and a private nook for reading and relaxing as a second smaller area. Screens, plants, furniture, and rugs can be arranged to define these smaller, more intimate areas.

Even when the room is large, do your best to locate activities such as work and exercise elsewhere in the house, or completely screen them from the bed. Sometimes, as in the "Follow your Bliss" story on page 205, it's best to turn a large master bedroom into a studio or office. In these cases, the abundance of space may be better suited for active, creative pursuits, while a smaller room lends itself to being a couple's bedroom oasis. Don't underestimate your instinctive need for coziness, nesting, warmth, and safety. Whatever size your master bedroom is, these needs remain.

**Encouraging Privacy:** Private times without children or telephones can be difficult to find in a couple's busy lifestyle. But it's one of the necessities of maintaining intimate contact with your partner. Each couple has to decide how to claim these private times, and when they're won, make sure they're supported by the bedroom's arrangement. Many couples discover a whole new intimacy, for instance, after moving photos of their children, parents, and friends *away* from the bed.

One couple had 25 photos of their four daughters "watching" them in bed. They rarely made love, and when they did, it was always in the dark or under the covers so that their daughters wouldn't "see" them! They moved the photos to the family room where they reigned over family activities, rather than over their parents' bedroom. As a result, the couple's love life greatly improved.

The same applies to religious art and figures. As meaningful as these items may be, they can color the mood of the bedroom. In one case, a couple's master bedroom was dominated by a large painting of the Virgin

Mary holding the infant Jesus. Both figures looked directly at the bed. Although they were a religious couple, they both relaxed and enjoyed a renewed intimacy in the bedroom when the painting was moved to the wife's sanctuary.

**Encouraging Equality and Unity:** The presence of nightstands, and the space allotted on each side of the bed, indicates equality or lack thereof in a couple's relationship. Many times I've heard a woman say that there is room for only one nightstand, and it's on her husband's side of the bed. As she's talking, I notice that his nightstand is twice as big as it needs to be! Changing this situation tends to change the dynamic between husband and wife, as well as the Ch'i flow in the room. And it can rustle some feathers. Symbolically, where one had previously ruled, two people and two spaces become equal. A nightstand and lamp on each side of the bed as well as enough room to get in and out is ideal. When space is limited, *both* partners need to scale down their bedside furniture.

**FIGURE 110**

*This couple has a very unpleasant view from the bed. He looks into the open toilet, and she looks at a very scary piece of art.*

**FIGURE 11P**

*The couple's view is improved and unified with a favorite romantic poster.*
*Magenta flannel sheets, fresh flowers, a candle, and a spring on the bathroom*
*door to keep it closed all create a warmer, more intimate atmosphere.*

**Encouraging Positive Points of View:** Couples who share the same positive view from the bed also tend to share the same positive viewpoints in life. Conversely, it is alarming to see what happens to couples when their views from the bed are very different and/or unpleasant.

One couple had particularly unfortunate views from their bed. Figure 11O shows the man's view through the open bathroom door into the toilet, while the woman looked at a graphically violent poster her husband had been given as a work-related memento. Together, they slept on ice-blue sheets. He was depressed, and she was nervous and edgy most of the time. And the loving connection they'd once felt had all but vanished.

When they realized the significance of their view from the bed, they put a soft spring on the bathroom door so it remained closed, and replaced the grisly art with a print of Gustav Klimt's "The Kiss," as shown in Figure 11P. They included a small table with a scented candle and a vase of fresh flowers. They also replaced their icy-blue bedding with a magenta flannel duvet and sheets. Almost immediately they noticed a positive change in their moods and in their interest in one another; the spark between them had a place to rekindle. My favorite part of their story is that before they enhanced their bedroom, they both wore flannel pajamas to bed. After they made the changes, they found that it was warm enough to sleep without their pajamas....

What you view from bed symbolizes the unity and connection—or lack thereof—you experience as a couple. When bathrooms and closets can be seen from the bed, pull the curtain or close the door on them before retiring. Concentrate on unifying and beautifying your view as this couple did, and enjoy the results.

**Encouraging Sensuality:** While every room in the house should please the senses, the master bedroom is the place that should glow with sensuality. Make it a place of soothing sounds; welcoming colors; pleasing art; soft, inviting fabrics; favorite fragrances; and delicious experiences. This is the place for you and your partner to relax and enjoy a sensual atmosphere.

Even people with the best intentions can take a wrong turn and leave sensuality in the dust. I worked with a couple who decided to create a chic monochromatic look in their bedroom by doing *everything* in one color—gray-green. This included their carpet, wall covering, window treatments, upholstery, bedspread, and sheets. They made the changes over a six-month period, and with every new gray-green addition, their relationship cooled down another notch. By the time the room was finished, the woman had moved into the guest room.

We talked at length about their color choice. Both had liked the look of a gray-green bedroom in a magazine photo, but when they thought about it, neither found the color to be warm or sensual. The more dominant the color had become, the less warmth and sensuality there was in the room—and between them. In fact, they were usually annoyed and "sick" of each other and had been for months. I asked them what colors they found sensual. They both immediately answered, "Pink!" The woman looked at her husband and asked in amazement, "You like *pink?*" In that moment, the pallor lifted, and they reconnected with a good laugh. Needless to say, they brought pink, and several other warm colors, into their once gray-green room, and as they restored the sensual balance in their bedroom, it was restored in their relationship.

**Encouraging Peace and Calm:** As shown in Figure 11M, put the TV behind closed doors in the master bedroom. Better yet, move it to another room. I've heard many people lament that since a TV had been moved into their bedroom, opportunities for lovemaking had all but moved out.

### Children's Bedrooms

Most of the children's bedrooms I see are neon bright and busy, busy, busy. It's no surprise when the parents remark that their child never settles down. In almost every case, the child is being overstimulated by the bedroom decor. Feng Shui observes a direct correlation between the epidemic of hyperactivity in our children and the way their bedrooms are decorated. When you really think about it, could you relax in a bedroom overflowing with toys and accentuated by bright primary colors and action figures swooping across every surface? This is a room that's perpetually awake and active. Instead, we need to tuck our children into the tranquil embrace of a cozy, serene bedroom that encourages them to calm down and get the rest they need.

**Colors to Sleep By:** When choosing colors for a child's bedroom, use the same color palette as described for all bedrooms on page 181. Replace bright primary colors such as fire-engine red, cobalt blue, and day-glow yellow with warm pastels or rich colors such as lavender, peach, butter cream, and cocoa. Change art and decorative themes that are flying, falling, driving, or running around the room to a motif that is tranquil and calm. Include self-esteem boosters that are frequently updated, such as a bulletin board for their latest creations, or easy-to-change frames displaying their artwork. Serenity is the keynote here. When you calm the bedroom down, you'll calm your child down, too.

**Possessions to Sleep By:** Children's bedrooms can easily become overcrowded with toys, games, equipment, and collections. Every item that speaks of activity contributes to keeping the room "awake." Display a selection of comfort toys, such as stuffed animals and dolls, and store their action-oriented toys out of sight in trunks, closets, and cabinets.

Children outgrow clothes, toys, and interests quickly, so it's an ongoing task to keep their possessions current. Teach your children that when they let go of the belongings they've lost interest in, they make room to receive the new things they'd really like to have.

**Family Photos, Mirrors, and Bedroom Pets:** Unlike the master bedroom, it's a good idea to keep family photos near the child's bed. Photographs of parents and other family members communicate love and security to a child. Children are often very sensitive to the activating influence of mirrors. Be sure to curtain, cover, or remove mirrors in their bedrooms, as shown in Figures 4N and 4O on page 83, especially when children aren't sleeping well.

Pets living in a child's bedroom, such as hamsters, lizards, turtles, and fish, need to be checked on a regular basis. It is not uncommon to see dank green aquariums or starving hamsters in bedrooms where the child had promised to take good care of them This is not only cruel to the pet, but it depletes the energy in the house. Keep an eye on your kids' pets, even when it's their responsibility to provide pet care.

**Siblings to Sleep By:** When children share a bedroom, give each child a distinct place within the room to call their own. It may be half of the room, a table and chair, a toy trunk, a closet, or a bureau. This keeps each child's individuality defined and helps them learn how to respect other people's space.

Bunk beds can be used as long as both children are happy with them. What may have been a snug retreat for a child can change—seemingly overnight—into a claustrophobic box as the child gets older. Be sensitive to children outgrowing their bunk beds, and rearrange the room accordingly.

**Children's Bedrooms and the Bagua Map:** I find that most children, including teens, really enjoy Feng Shui. They love the idea of the Bagua Map (Chapter 2) and often use it to enhance the personal domain of their bedrooms. A client's 12-year-old daughter "Feng Shuied" her own bedroom by straightening her closet, putting her piggy bank in the Wealth and Prosperity area, and giving away toys she'd lost interest in. Immediately, she attracted opportunities in her life, including several pet-sitting jobs in her neighborhood. She was thrilled to have a chance to care for neighbors' pets, demonstrate her dependability, and earn some extra money. And as we so often observe in Feng Shui, this rippled out to attract more goodness into her life, including the pride and appreciation of her parents and neighbors, as well as more fun jobs.

To teenagers, the Bagua Map is "the Grid" that shows them how to arrange their bedrooms to create positive results in their lives. One of my clients called almost in tears because, for the first time in four years, her 16-year-old daughter had cleaned up her room. Why? She wanted to "do the Grid," and cleaning it up was the first step. She then rearranged her bedroom and put her school books into the Knowledge and Self-Cultivation area, and her art supplies into Creativity and Children. Her mom said her daughter's whole attitude improved, along with her grades and social life.

### Single People's Bedrooms

Taking action on the suggestions previously discussed will certainly help prepare your bedroom for a lover. Experience has shown me, however, that single men and women sometimes unknowingly arrange their bedrooms to hold their singleness in place. If you are "In Search Of," make sure your bedroom is in alignment with your intentions.

**FIGURE 11Q**
*This bedroom, although appealing in many ways, holds a woman's single status in place. The single horse is perpetually galloping away in the Love and Marriage area of the room. The doll and delicate pillows "protect" the bed, and suggest that it's already taken. The teddy bear in the chair, the single-woman statue on the bureau, the "one night stand," and the lamp all symbolize aloneness. And the white gauzy curtain suggests that bandages are needed for injuries from past love affairs. (**Also in color, page 122.**)*

**FIGURE 11R**

*The bedroom is now inviting romance. Delicate pillows, the doll, teddy bear, horse, statue, and gauze curtain have been removed. Candles, flowers, a second nightstand and lamp, deep red linens, and an area rug have been added. Best of all, the Love and Marriage area is now enhanced with a sensual sculpture by Ert'e. (Also in color, page 123.)*

**Single Ladies—Preparing to Receive Love:** Prepare your bedroom to appeal to your new lover. Invite romance into your life by setting up your bedroom for two. Put nightstands and lamps on both sides of your bed, and make sure that there's sufficient space to walk around without bumping into things—even if *tonight* you are the only one there.

As is the case with other rooms, large numbers of accent pillows can be too much of a good thing. Pillows that have to be carefully removed before you can use the bed become more of a barrier than an enhancement to romance. Most men don't like delicate accent pillows, viewing them as prissy little annoyances that require special handling. If you can't throw them down or ball them up under your head, pillows are often perceived as a nuisance. A couple of easy-care accent pillows on your bed is plenty.

Remove dolls and stuffed animal "guardians" from the bed. These bed guards symbolically take the space meant for your lover and can be construed as tokens of an unfinished childhood or emotional inaccessibility.

Whatever their message, they hinder romantic spontaneity. Likewise, remove photos of past lovers from your bedroom. Act as if your lover is already in your life by designing an inviting bedroom and an approachable, sensuous bed that the two of you can enjoy without a "single" care.

Art depicting solitary subjects such as a single flower, a woman alone, or one animal perpetually affirm being alone. Good examples of these are in Figure 11Q. Instead, bring in art depicting pairs of subjects. I have worked with many women who unknowingly held their single life in place by filling their homes with art depicting one subject, often a woman looking lonely, aloof, angry, or sad. One client had more than 20 framed posters and cards of solitary women on her bedroom walls. Every night she slept alone with her 20-some lone companions. When you want to attract romance, change your onesomes to twosomes (as shown in Figure 11R and 11S) that inspire you, such as pairs of people, animals, flowers, trees, or a sculpture. Or group pairs of favorite items—candlesticks, vases, statuary, flowers, and books—around the house, especially in the Love and Marriage area (see the Bagua Map, Chapter 2) of your home and bedroom to further energize your desire and intention to be romantically involved.

**FIGURE 11S**

*Sensual sculpture by Ert'e brings an air of romance into the bedroom.* ***(Also in color, page 124.)***

Whether single or married, the most important step you can take is to have a love affair with yourself. Create an enchanting bedroom atmosphere with scented candles or oils, music that soothes you, and colors and fabrics that make you melt. Strengthen your charisma by opening your heart fully to yourself, knowing that the right lover will appear at the right time. Build your capacity to love and be loved by loving yourself *now*. Affirm: *"I love, honor, and celebrate my life, now and always. My loving thoughts, words, and actions increase my magnetism and strengthen the heartbeat of joy and happiness within me."*

**FIGURE 11T**

*This single man's bedroom includes many Feng Shui challenges, including bed placement, exercise equipment, bedside art of a lonely man, one lamp and nightstand, a partner-eating plant, and a general lack of order. The large white painting by Richard Haeger is lost in a white room dominated by the Metal element. (Also in color, page 125.)*

**FIGURE 11U**

*Changes include moving the bed to a solid wall, adding a colorful painting by Sally Pearce, red rugs, and a second nightstand and lamp. Luxurious linens warm up the bed, while a red candle, a table by Charles Thomas, and sculpture by Karin Swildens enhance the Love and Marriage area. A healthy new palm accents the Wealth and Prosperity area. **(Also in color, page 125.)***

**Single Gentlemen:** Single men's bedrooms are often "command stations" where the bed is crowded in among other functional items such as a desk, computer, filing cabinet, television, stereo, and exercise equipment. Lovers don't line up at the door that leads to this kind of bedroom. I worked with a single man whose bedroom was so chaotic and crowded with furniture, boxes, and equipment that it took me a few minutes to locate the bed. He wondered why he never had a girlfriend for very long. It turns out that as soon as any woman saw his bedroom, she ran the other way.

To attract and keep a lover, let the bed rule your bedroom. When at all possible, locate your desk, exercise equipment, TV, and computer in another room, or screen them from the bed when not in use. Beautiful art, sensuous linens, and warm colors should all say, "Come on in and make yourself at home."

This was the goal of a man who was determined to change his single status. Figure 11T shows his bedroom before any changes were made. The bed was under the window, the exercise bike co-ruled the room and doubled as a towel rack, and the reading chair was buried under piles of clothes. His one nightstand included a picture of a single guy who looked like he'd lost all his luck, while the other side of the bed was possessed by a giant palm tree. White linens, nightstands, walls, and a painting, along with metal exercise equipment, meant that the room was dominated by the Metal element. Interestingly, he was "always in his head," and hadn't been romantically involved for a long time.

He moved his bed to a solid wall and exchanged the large white painting for a colorful lightweight piece that brought in the Fire and Wood elements, as shown in Figure 11U. He removed the massive palm, added several deep red rugs, and bought *two* bed lamps with leopard print shades for his nightstands. He splurged on linens and other enhancements for his romantic hideaway. The table, sculpture, and candle complement the Love and Marriage area, while a new palm of appropriate size enhances the Wealth and Prosperity area. From cold and disorganized to warm and inviting, the man's bedroom symbolized his love life. Within weeks of completing his bedroom, a friendship with a woman he'd known for years blossomed into a promising romance.

**Letting Go of the Past and Luxuriating in the Present:** Lovers love luxurious linens. You can count on sensual bedding making a positive impression. Linens that are threadbare, clashing, or marked with the scent of the past will not help you win your lover. I recently worked with a single man who was still using the linens his ex-wife had bought during their marriage more than a decade ago. Now, after many years of use, they were quite threadbare. In addition, they broke every Feng Shui rule, being a faded half-polyester navy blue. Their condition was a signal to any perceptive woman that this man's past marriage was still stamped upon the bedroom, and therefore, on him.

When I asked him what memories were associated with the linens, he was flooded with a new awareness. He had learned as a child to keep possessions until they were completely worn out. He'd felt lucky when his estranged wife had left the linens. Now, he realized that his inability to fully let go of the past and attract a new romantic relationship was all wrapped up in his sheets. It was time for him to get rid of "the blues" and arrange his bedroom to express his own unique tastes.

He chose high thread-count Egyptian cotton sheets and a bedspread in burnished bronze and gold. To complement them, he enlarged and framed several photographs of the undulant California hills cast in the golden light of sunset. The effect was quite marvelous in his bedroom and in his love life. He met and is enjoying dating several attractive women. But best of all, he's discovered how much he enjoys his own company.

**Art That Attracts a Lover:** To attract a new love into your life, remove unframed posters, magazine centerfolds, or art depicting violence from your bedroom. Lovers almost never "get it," and instead, get *out*. Set the tone and the mood by introducing artistic elements that suggest sensuality and serenity. It may be a landscape, where hilly curves suggest hips or shoulders, or a waterscape, where sailboats convey pleasure and relaxation. Sensual sculptures, a collection of candles, fresh flowers, and healthy plants can also create an invitingly romantic atmosphere. They will be noticed and appreciated.

### Guest Rooms

A guest room is a luxury that some homes are blessed with. When you have the space for a dedicated guest room, be sure to include it as an equal member of your household. Leave the door open, and design it so that it pleases you every time you see it. Don't let it become a chaotic storage area, as it will negatively affect the Ch'i flow in your home.

Give your guest room the same serene elements of comfort that your own bedroom has. Make plenty of room in the closet and drawers for your visitors' belongings. Provide a place for unpacking and storing a suitcase or two. Include the little comforts and conveniences you would like to be greeted with, such as warm robes and scented toiletries. Happy guests enhance the energy in your home. Give your guest room a personality that invites your visitors to relax and enjoy their stay.

A guest room is also one of the easiest rooms in the house to claim for other needs and interests. It can be redesigned to be a home office

(Chapter 10), exercise room, or sanctuary (Chapter 12). Don't compromise your own work performance or personal needs all year long when you can claim a room that's used only occasionally for guests. And when it's arranged to serve another purpose, you can still incorporate a place for guests to sleep, such as a Murphy bed, day bed, Hide-a-Bed, or futon.

**Inviting Success to Be Your Guest:** Positive change can occur when you assess your special needs through Feng Shui eyes. In one case, two men who lived together shared one home office. They both felt cramped in a space that offered no visual or auditory privacy, and they noticed that this was beginning to strain their relationship. Meanwhile, sitting silently across the hall was a guest room.

Until our Feng Shui appointment, it hadn't occurred to them to claim the guest room as a second office. Both men's families came to visit from time to time, and they had assumed they needed to reserve a room exclusively for guests. However, their work needs now outweighed the luxury of keeping a dedicated guest room that remained vacant most of the time. They could see how the chronic congestion in one room could be eased by turning the guest room into a second office. They each picked a room and spread out. For guests, they bought a futon for one office, and a large reading chair that converted into a single bed for the other.

They barely had their phones straightened out when their careers took off. They now had plenty of space to grow and develop their businesses, and it showed. More than a year later, they are experiencing more success and happiness than ever.

### QUICK REFERENCE GUIDELINES FOR BEDROOMS

- Place your bed so that you can see the door.
- Move desks and exercise equipment to other rooms, or screen them from the bed.
- Either have no television in your bedroom at all, or put it into a cabinet or armoire.
- Drape mirrors at night, or remove them from the room.
- Select natural, sensuous linens.
- Choose skin tones and warm, rich colors.

- Create a beautiful view from the bed.
- Bring in sensual or serene art.
- Honor the five senses.
- Apply the Bagua Map, and balance the Five Elements.

*Chapter Twelve*

# THE SANCTUARY—
# ROOM FOR THE SPIRIT

*"In order to give back to our relationships, careers,
families, and passions, we must pull in for short
moments to take care of ourselves . . ."*
— Chris Casson Madden

A sanctuary is a room dedicated to the exploration of your passions and interests. It may be a place of complete quiet and peace, devoted to yoga, healing, writing, or meditation, or it may take the form of an art or dance studio. Although it usually doesn't exist in the typical home blueprint, just about any room or space—including a guest room, dining room, den, bedroom, basement, attic, garage, or library—can be made into a sanctuary. In this special place, you are utterly free to express yourself, whether it's making art, playing music, singing, dancing, dreaming, meditating, or writing. Claim any little-used room as a sanctuary in your home, and give it a whole new identity—one that supports your personal growth and development.

**FIGURE 12A**

*This sanctuary is dedicated to meditation and healing. The altar features mean-ingful objects, books, flowers, and candles. (See the close-up in Figure 4V on page 116.)*

**FIGURE 12B**

*The sanctuary in Figure 12A leads to an outdoor meditation deck built around a tree and enhanced with plants, flowers, and an amethyst geode.*

### Follow Your Bliss

When a client named Linda became involved with her local theater, she needed a place at home to rehearse. She and her husband, Kevin, lived in a house that had a huge master bedroom suite and two small bedrooms, used as guest room and office. Linda realized that she couldn't move around freely in either of the small bedrooms, and the acoustics were terrible. She needed more space! After looking over the situation, we decided that it would be ideal to turn the master bedroom into her sanctuary/studio and move their bedroom into the guest room. Kevin agreed to this rather unconventional idea as an experiment. He wanted to be sure he liked the change before he gave it his long-term stamp of approval.

Linda and Kevin discovered that it worked better than they thought possible. They reorganized the closets, left her clothes in the master bedroom, and outfitted the closet in the home office for his clothes. Instead of tip-toeing around in the morning in an effort not to wake Linda up, Kevin now had his own dressing room. Meanwhile, the master suite gave Linda plenty of space to move around, and the large mirrored closet doors were perfect for dance practice. And, cozily tucked into the nest of their little bedroom, they were no longer awakened at the crack of dawn by the light reflected in a wall of mirrors. Both had noticed how much better they were sleeping as a result. Although it surprised them and many of their friends, this arrangement met their needs beautifully.

**FIGURE 12C**

*A dance floor and mirrors installed in a spare bedroom create a sanctuary for a young woman majoring in choreography.*

## *Claiming Your Space*

I have found that couples and families are happiest when every family member has a space or sanctuary to call their own. Figure 12D shows a home office/sanctuary, where personal memorabilia that other family members have no interest in can be proudly displayed. When our personal needs are met in this way, compromising on the design and arrangement of shared areas usually becomes a much easier process.

**FIGURE 12D**

*This room combines a home office with a sanctuary. The desk is placed near the front of the room with a view of the door, while the couch provides a place to relax and read. This man's personal memorabilia, including mementos from his military service and a drum made during a health retreat, find a home here.*

### QUICK REFERENCE GUIDELINES FOR THE SANCTUARY

- Dedicate it to your personal growth and development.
- Design and arrange it to be an intimate reflection of you.
- Use the Five Elements and Bagua Map as needed.

# *Chapter Thirteen*

# BATHROOMS—
# CLEANSING WATERS

*"The bathroom is a body temple, the place where we
retreat ritually several times a day to reconnect with our
physical nature—to experience bodily cycles, to enjoy our
naked skin, to bathe languidly in warm water, or invigorate ourselves with a brisk shower."*

— Carol Venolia

There's some humor in the fact that this chapter is number 13.
"Chapter 13," a synonym for bankruptcy, reminds me of the popular
Feng Shui belief that bathrooms create financial problems. The phrase, "I
might as well have flushed my money down the toilet," sums it up.
Bathroom plumbing is thought to literally drain vital energy and
resources from the house. But if you design your bathrooms to be as
pleasant and uplifting as they are functional, this doesn't have to be the
case. With Feng Shui, you can keep the energy balanced and flowing
through your bathrooms and your bank accounts.

### Close the Drains or Close the Doors

Begin by keeping the drains closed when not in use. Although especially important with the toilet because of its large opening, all drains can
pull the Ch'i down to some extent. Pull the sink, shower, and bathtub

stoppers closed when you're not using them, or cover the drains with small rubber mats made for that purpose.

When all else fails, at least keep the bathroom door closed. This is easily accomplished by putting the door on a soft spring so that it opens easily and closes softly behind you. This will also preserve the Ch'i flow throughout the rest of the house.

If your bedroom leads to a bathroom without a door, make it a priority to install a door, curtain, or screen to visually separate the bathroom from the bedroom, as shown in Figures 11H and 11I on page 177. Along with assuring privacy and visual serenity, this also assures good energy flow in each room.

Ideally, a toilet is placed so that you don't see it from the bathroom door. Locate it in its own "water closet" or behind a wall or screen. When this is impossible, hang a round faceted cut-glass crystal from the ceiling between the door and the toilet, as shown in Figure 4E, page 72, to help lift and circulate the Ch'i.

### Meaningful Motifs

Make all bathrooms beautiful! You will quickly lift the Ch'i with a fresh coat of paint, new bathroom linens, candles, art, and plants. If a bathroom has little or no natural light, include a low-wattage lamp or night-light, and keep it lit most or all of the time, as shown in Figure 13A. Small bathrooms appear larger and more welcoming when you choose wallpaper or art that has depth. Bring items into the bathroom that you love to see, and keep the counters, bath area, and cabinets free of clutter. And bury those "dead soldiers"— shampoo and other cosmetic bottles that are almost empty or too old to use.

When deciding on bathroom colors and motifs, take the Five Elements (Chapter 3) into consideration. Elementally speaking, the bathroom is very Watery and can be balanced by adding elements associated with Earth, such as yellow or earthy colors, earthenware items, and ceramic tiles. The Fire element, which "makes" and strengthens Earth, also brings in warmth and light via candles, lamps, fiery colors, and art depicting animals or people. And, because the Wood element "drinks" Water and "feeds" Fire, you can enhance your bathroom with healthy plants, fresh flowers, art that portrays gardens, floral or striped wallpaper and towels, wooden items, and blues and greens. Figure 4D on page is an example of a small bathroom that has been balanced with Earth, Fire, and Wood touches. The Metal element, associated with white, stone, and metallic items, isn't accentuated, as it tends to hold, and therefore strengthen, the already dominant Water element. The idea is to strike a balance with what had been an extremely Watery room.

**FIGURE 13A**

*Many Ch'i enhancements including red walls, a plant, art, luxurious towels, and a low-wattage lamp that's always on keep the Ch'i buoyant in this windowless bathroom.*
***(Also in color, page 126.)***

### *Bathroom Bagua*

Also consider what part of the Bagua Map your bathroom is located in, and tailor your motif to match. The Wealth and Prosperity area, just like any other Bagua area, can "land" in your bathroom. When a client realized that her Wealth and Prosperity area was in the scruffy back bathroom she never used, she transformed it by hanging rich burgundy-red curtains next to the tub, changing all the towels to match the curtains, and adding luxurious accessories. It quickly became the most popular bathroom in the house, and more prosperity than ever flowed into her household.

**FIGURE 13B**

*This bathroom is located in the Love and Marriage area of the house. An arched alcove, flowers, and a floral border by mural artist Jacki Powell all give the room a romantic flair. Other enhancements include pink towels, scented oil lamps, and bath oils.*

You can make a bathroom in the Wealth and Prosperity area richly opulent; a Love and Marriage bathroom sensual and fragrant (as shown in Figure 13B); and a Health and Family bathroom bright and cheery with floral art and accessories. No matter where it is located, if your bathroom is a beautiful place that has its own special ambience, it will assure good Ch'i flow.

## CONTEMPLATIVE EXERCISE

BATHROOMS SYMBOLIZE CLEANSING AND LETTING GO OF THE OLD TO MAKE ROOM FOR THE NEW. MAKE SURE YOU AREN'T HOLDING ON TO OLD ATTITUDES THAT KEEP YOU FROM FEELING THE JOY AND PROMISE OF EACH NEW MOMENT. CHECK FOR "TOXIC" PATTERNS OF THINKING AND FEELING, SUCH AS RESENTMENT, ANGER, OR POWER-LESSNESS. THEN, DURING YOUR NEXT SHOWER OR BATH, CONSCIOUS-LY RELEASE THEM INTO THE CLEANSING WATERS. LET THEM GO RIGHT DOWN THE DRAIN WITH THE SOAPY WATER. WHILE WASHING YOUR BODY, YOU CAN ALWAYS INCLUDE THE DEEPER CLEANSING OF UNHAP-PY OR UNHEALTHY THOUGHTS AND EMOTIONS SO THAT YOU REMAIN SPARKLING CLEAN, INSIDE AND OUT.

### QUICK REFERENCE GUIDELINES FOR BATHROOMS

- Keep all drains closed when not in use.
- When possible, screen the toilet from the door.
- Put a door, curtain, or screen between the bedroom and bathroom.
- Balance bathrooms according to the Five Elements and the Bagua Map.
- Make all of your bathrooms beautiful and clutter-free.

# Chapter Fourteen

# LAUNDRY ROOMS AND GARAGES— DIAMONDS IN THE ROUGH

*"The garage to most of us is our enclosed junkyard–kind of a giant seasoning cellar for our debatable belongings."*
— Don Aslett

## *The Laundry Room*

In most homes, laundry rooms are considered non-rooms, and, like storage rooms, garages, and basements, are often cluttered, poorly lit, and unadorned. Because every room is considered equal in Feng Shui, it's important to make your laundry room as pleasant as every other room in your home.

Laundry rooms are best located near the bedrooms, where most laundry is generated. They should be spacious enough to include places for storing laundry supplies, an iron and ironing board (if you use one), and a sorting and hanging area. If your laundry room is also a second foyer next to the garage or back door, as in Figure 14A, display symbols that you enjoy seeing every time you leave or enter the house. When you can, house your washer and dryer in a closet or behind a screen or curtain so that they can be visually put away between uses.

**FIGURE 14A**

*Bright sunflowers in this laundry room welcome owners home as they come in through the garage.*

Whether it's an entrance or not, your laundry room is a place where you can be as playful and colorful as you'd like in choosing accents. Check the Bagua Map (Chapter 2) to see what area your laundry room is located in so you can set a theme for its decor. Display things that you love, but which may not fit in other rooms, such as posters of rock 'n' roll or sports stars, college memorabilia, or your child's finger paintings. Consider painting the laundry room door—or the laundry room itself—a wild and crazy color. Or, you may want to really break tradition and bring things into the laundry room not normally found there. Anything that makes you feel good enhances the Ch'i. Brighten it up with a crystal chandelier, a fabulous mirror, or a collection of antique glass. Sorting and folding your laundry takes on a whole new meaning when you're sur-rounded with fun or beautiful things. Give the laundry room flair and personality so that you smile every time you see it.

## *The Garage*

**FIGURE 14B**

*While chaos rules the garage, automobiles are relegated to the street. This out-of-control garage symbolizes the owners' feelings of being out of control in life.*

**FIGURE 14C**

*Taking control of the garage breathes vitality into every aspect of life. After throwing away or donating most of the stuff in the garage, the owner organized the rest on existing shelves and moved the cars back in. Now the junk is gone, and the truly valuable possessions have a home. A director's chair and a framed photo of a white tiger act as greeters at the garage entry to the house.*

**FIGURE 14D**

*This garage, called the "car room" by the owner, has been painted to match the rest of the house, and is enhanced with cabinets, artwork, and flowers.*

The simple, unfinished design of most garages dates back to a time when our transportation was housed in barns and stables. Horses and carriages were located in a building apart from the house. It was, and still is, a good idea to locate transportation in another building, as it assures good air quality and a more peaceful flow of Ch'i in the house. It also keeps dangerous car fumes and transient garage activities away from you and your family. As land becomes more valuable and our love for convenience grows, however, garages are often attached to the house. This poses some Feng Shui challenges.

When the garage is attached to your home, leave the garage door open for a few minutes after turning off the car so that fumes don't enter the house. Rooms located above or beside the garage are influenced by the garage's transient energy and are best used for work or play activities, rather than bedrooms.

Along with safety and comfort issues, your garage needs to be kept neat and organized. (This also applies to a detached garage as well as any other "out building" on your property.) Whenever you feel confused or overwhelmed in the garage, you know that it's time to shovel it out and return it to order. Always leave plenty of space to maneuver your car in and out without hitting toys, sports equipment, or a growing pile of garage sale items. I've been in garages where there was barely enough room to park, open the car door, and squeeze through the piles of stuff to get into the house. Then there are garages such as the one shown in Figure 14B where no parking spot remains. Even with the door kept shut, chaos like this stagnates the Ch'i, and inevitably has a negative impact on the owners' lives.

When organizing the garage, set up specific areas for storage, and for activities such as potting plants, making crafts, and working with engines or wood. Treat yourself to all the shelves and containers you need to organize the space. As Figure 14C shows, it doesn't have to be fancy; it just needs to be organized so that you know where everything is. If necessary, rent a storage locker to house items that are taking up precious space, and tell your friends and relatives to do the same! Your garage is *not* their storage locker. And, please, have the garage sale you've been planning for months or years *now*. By getting rid of the things you no longer want or need, you revitalize your home, and make room for what you really *do* want to flow into your life.

Along with organizing your garage, give it some personality, as shown in Figure 14D. Hang posters or other pleasing elements there; paint it your favorite color; use the carpeting you replaced in another room to soften the floor; install plenty of lighting; or transform it into an art studio, family room, or office. Check your garage's location on the Bagua Map (Chapter 2), and choose enhancements that correlate with that area. Any enhancements that please you will strengthen the Ch'i flowing through your home.

**QUICK REFERENCE GUIDELINES FOR THE LAUNDRY ROOM AND GARAGE**

- Treat the laundry room and garage like any other room in your home.
- Make them appealing by decorating them to your taste.
- Obtain necessary shelving and cabinets to keep them organized.
- Avoid the tendency to allow excess possessions to accumulate there.

# *Chapter Fifteen*

# ATTICS, BASEMENTS, AND OTHER STORAGE AREAS— GIVING EVERYTHING A HOME

*"It's discouraging to think that a bunch of clutter could cheat us out of our future—a vibrant, zestful, rapture-filled life. It can! It is!"*
— Don Aslett

When I think of attics and basements, I think of darkness. I grew up in a house that had both an attic and a basement, and both were poorly lit. I remember waving my hand around in the pitch black looking for the light pull at the top of the attic stairs. Once I found the string, a bare light bulb dimly lit a small area around the stairs, leaving the rest of the attic in darkness.

The basement was worse. There I had to walk through inky darkness to the far wall where the light switches were. My imagination always got the better of me as I hurried through the darkness, and by the time I got to the switches, my heart would be thumping wildly. This was not "good Feng Shui." Lighting, a bright symbol of safety and comfort, did not have a home in our dark, spooky attic and basement. Meanwhile, on the main floor of the house, where the "real rooms" were, lamps illuminated every room.

My family's attic and basement were not unusual. All of my friends had equally scary and dangerous basements, attics, and storerooms where chaos reigned in the darkness. These were the indoor dumps where extra, old, seasonal, and broken stuff could get thrown without a second thought. Most homes were very presentable until we got to the storage areas. Then the overwhelming chaos made it difficult to even move, let alone find anything.

### Enlighten Your Belongings

Although this is a new concept to our Western way of thinking, storage areas such as attics and basements need to be honored as equals in the family of rooms that make up your home. When dark and cluttered, they become unhealthy pockets that zap your home's vitality. Light your storage areas, as well as any other room in your house. This is one of the easiest ways to lift and invigorate these spaces. Locate light switches and night-lights conveniently, and in the presence of all that illumination, unclutter and organize the entire space, making sure that whatever lives there is loved or useful in some way. This includes holiday paraphernalia, gift wrapping, furniture, books, papers, clothes, tools, art supplies, papers, and memorabilia. Make these items easy to find and retrieve by labeling and storing them within reach and out of harm's way. Give our possessions—*all of them*—a good home. Storage areas need to be refreshed and reorganized at least once a year, since what you decided to keep last year—from tax papers to Grandma's coat rack—may be ready to go now.

When you arrange your storage areas to be pleasant and organized—with every possession well cared for—the quality of life, including your creativity and peace of mind, will be greatly enhanced. Remember, your environment displays your consciousness, and there's no more revealing place to look than in your storage areas.

### Mess-engers in the Storeroom

My life presented me with a wonderful opportunity to learn how tricky storage areas can be. Brian and I live on property that includes two beach cottages. Most of our living quarters are in the front cottage, including our living and dining room, kitchen, and two home offices. Our master bedroom is in the back cottage, along with guest quarters and a storeroom. One night we noticed the patter of little feet nearby, and we quickly discovered that our storeroom had become the home for several families of rodents known as Norwegian fruit rats. Although smaller and cuter than other types of rats, they were quickly making a mess of things and needed to be removed.

Before their appearance, I had been under the impression that our storeroom was just fine—a little disorderly, perhaps, but hey, we're busy people (sound familiar?). We'd get around to straightening it up some-time soon. When the fruit rats demanded that I really take a detailed look, I was startled by the amount of junk that had built up while we weren't looking. No wonder the rats liked it so much—the place was a disaster area!

Unfortunately, the rats gave us no slack. They didn't wait for us to schedule a convenient time to deal with them and the storeroom they now inhabited. In one day, they chewed a hole through the wall of the storeroom into our bedroom. There, they were caught in broad daylight feasting upon Payday and Million Dollar candy bars—whimsical Wealth and Prosperity symbols given to me by friends. My arrival signaled an abrupt end to their party, and they raced across the bed to get back to "their" storeroom.

Thoroughly alarmed (and slightly amused), I realized that we couldn't put off this situation another minute. We were being forced to *pay attention*! We dropped everything and emptied out our storeroom to dis-cover that most of what was there, including furniture, suitcases, clothes, papers, and books, was useless to us now. Over the next few days, we filled two pick-up trucks with "junk" for a friend's garage sale. We recycled over 250 pounds of old business papers, bought 37 large plastic contain-ers to organize the things we wanted to keep in storage, and in the process, found and closed the "door" where the fruit rats were getting in.

The cleaning frenzy that started in the storeroom ignited throughout both cottages. We searched every room for things that no longer belonged in our lives. This resulted in another six boxes of "good stuff" for the garage sale. A giddy feeling of relief filled us as we cleared each room. Surrounded *exclusively* by the things we loved, we swept away any heaviness from the past and reveled in the clarity of the moment. And, as is so often the case, new work and social opportunities tumbled into our lives.

I still chuckle when I think of those little fruit rats feasting on my sweet symbols of wealth and prosperity. What a gift they were!

### QUICK REFERENCE GUIDELINES FOR STORAGE AREAS

- Include plenty of lighting.
- Keep these areas pleasant and organized by giving all stored items a good home.
- Reorganize at least once a year.
- Check these rooms frequently for Creeping Chaos, and treat immediately.

# *Chapter Sixteen*

# HALLWAYS AND STAIRWAYS—
# CONNECTING PASSAGEWAYS

*"Unless a staircase is made to live,
it will be a dead spot, and work to disconnect
the building and tear its processes apart."*
— Christopher Alexander

Hallways and stairways connect the rooms and floors of our homes and are the passageways through which we, along with the vital energy that nurtures our homes, travel. However, in many cases, they are extreme in their character and need to be balanced and enhanced to channel a healthy flow of Ch'i.

## *Hallways*

Hallways are frequently dark and plain. The longer, thinner, and darker they are, the more people feel compelled to hurry through them. In Feng Shui, we want to encourage the opposite and slow people down to a healthy pace. We do this by making the hall a pleasant, interesting place to be.

**FIGURE 16A**

*Art with depth, such as this nature scene by artist Jeff Kahn, opens up the wall across from a hall door.*

**FIGURE 16B**

*Bookshelves, lighting, and art transform this hall into an attractive place where people can enjoy the many items of interest.*

Approach your hallway as a "room" with unique qualities. For instance, its long, thin shape lends itself to being an art gallery where you can display paintings, photographs, posters, mirrors, or other collectibles along the walls. Each piece acts as a "window," bringing color and interest to the hall. Skylights and track lighting can add a dramatic touch, transforming a long, dark space into a bright salon. To open up and brighten views, hang mirrors or art with depth directly across from doors that enter into a hallway, as shown in Figure 16A. Conversely, the end of a long corridor is enhanced by art with no depth, such as a still life that accents the space without appearing to lengthen the hall.

When the hall is wide enough, punctuate it with furniture, carpets, plants, and other items that pleasantly appoint the space. A hallway can be the perfect place for a library, with bookshelves and accent lighting providing plenty of interest, as shown in Figure 16B. Don't overcrowd a hallway in an effort to make it more interesting! Be sure that your choices enhance, not obstruct, Ch'i flow.

Faceted crystals are also used to help circulate and balance the energy in hallways. They can be hung unobtrusively a few inches below the hall ceiling, at about ten-foot intervals. Or use crystal light fixtures to provide light and crystalline enhancement.

### Stairways

Stairways are often seen in Feng Shui as "rushing waterfalls,"which channel energy too quickly from one floor to another. They are especially challenging when they fall directly toward a home's front entrance, rushing the Ch'i meant to nurture the occupants' health and good fortune down and out of the house. Here, the vital energy entering the door is flowing "against the tide" and is swept back out before it has had a chance to meander through the house. Wherever they are located, the longer and steeper the stairs, the more in need of balance they are. When building stairways, face them away from doors, especially the front door, and make them wide and gracious, with risers and landings to modulate Ch'i flow.

**FIGURE 16C**

*A small cabinet defines the landing, while a mirror by Dan Diaz catches the descending Ch'i and keeps it circulating. Both enhancements are also functional, providing occupants with a place for keys and a glimpse of themselves before leaving the house.*

**FIGURE 16D**

*Art with an uplifting quality, such as this floral painting by Jacki Powell, raises and balances the Ch'i in the stairwell.*

When working with an existing stairway, place attractive items near the base of the stairs, such as a sculpture, screen, furniture (Figure 16C), water features, or plants. Just make sure your choices don't crowd the area. A faceted crystal above the bottom step also helps to lift and circulate the falling Ch'i.

When space is limited, hang a mirror directly across from the stairs, as in Figure 16C, to symbolically catch the descending rush of energy and reflect it back up the stairs. Artwork that has an uplifting quality (Figure

16D) is another good choice. Or stabilize the stairway itself by hanging a beautiful cloth over the banister (Figure 16F). By adding interest and beauty to the stairs, you will help balance the flow of vital energy throughout your home.

**FIGURE 16E**

*Here is a stairway descending from a small foyer. Even the cat is reluctant to take the plunge.*

**FIGURE 16F**

*To balance the stairway, owners hung art to create a strong horizontal plane that counters the verticality of the stairs. The foyer is stabilized and made more welcoming with handwoven cloth and flowers. The chair below has been moved to give the occupant a peripheral view of the door and to direct energy into the living room. A crystal hangs over the bottom stair to balance Ch'i circulation.*

When you hang art in a descending order down the stairwell, you accentuate the stair's descent. Instead, use art to create a strong horizontal line by hanging one or more framed pieces at the same height in the stairwell, as shown in Figure 16F. This is similar to establishing the line between heaven and earth (page 130). Art that has a buoyant, uplifting quality—such as trees, birds in flight, and people smiling or dancing—are recommended, as well as art composed of mostly horizontal lines.

Spiral staircases are also viewed as extreme features in Feng Shui. Their corkscrew shape channels Ch'i down like a giant drain, and the lack of risers whisks Ch'i out in every direction. Hence, spiral staircases can feel dangerous, much like a whirlpool. To balance the down-and-out pull, accentuate the central pole by painting it a different color than the rest of the staircase. Because spiral stairs suggest the movement of Water, consider painting the central pole blue or green to strengthen the Wood element, and the stairs an earthtone color to bring in the element of Earth. Or, you might place healthy plants that grow upward (Wood) in terra-cotta pots (Earth) around the base of the stairs.

### QUICK REFERENCE GUIDELINES FOR HALLWAYS AND STAIRWAYS

- Keep hallways and stairways open and clear of items that block easy passage.
- When possible, appoint with art, bookshelves, furniture, rugs, plants, and other enhancements.
- Match enhancements to Bagua locations.
- Use art, mirrors, and crystals to balance Ch'i flow.

# Chapter Seventeen

# WINDOWS AND DOORS—
# THE EYES AND MOUTHS
# OF THE HOME

*"We discover that windows and entrances unfold into special places for joining the inside and the outside, the public and the private, places for the ceremonies of greeting and saying goodbye. We rediscover the specialness and infinite variety of window seats and doorsteps that occur when the two different worlds touch."*
— Thomas Bender

## Windows

Windows are considered the eyes of the house. They bring light and views into your home, and their placement and treatment is important when adjusting the flow of air and Ch'i throughout.

When building, it's best not to put a door directly across from a window (or door), especially a large picture window with an awesome view, as this tends to pull the energy too quickly through the room. Attractive as it may be, it can overstimulate people while leaving the room "undernourished." Ideally, we—as well as the Ch'i—have a moment to adjust and settle into a room before we're pulled through to the other side. And views are often more enticing when discovered rather than immediately apparent.

**FIGURE 17A**

*A sculpture on a pedestal helps to slow and circulate the Ch'i streaming through the front door to the back windows.*

**FIGURE 17B**

*The simple addition of a faceted crystal in a window can balance the flow of Ch'i through a room.*

When you have a large window and a door lined up directly across from each other, place something attractive between them, such as an aquarium, plants, flowers, or sculpture, as shown in Figure 17A. Curtains, furniture, plants, and art placed near the window can also help slow and redirect some of the energy passing through the room. When there is no space for these things, hang a round, faceted crystal in the window, as shown in Figure 17B, or midway between window and door.

**FIGURE 17C**

*A piece of garden statuary and plants create an inspiring view outside a window.*

**FIGURE 17D**

*Arrange intimate views with beauty marks, such as this angel birdbath and seasonal flowers outside the home office, kitchen, bedroom, and bathroom windows.*
**(Also in color, page 127.)**

Check the view you have from every window (and door) in your home. What do you see? If you love what you see, great. If you don't, decide what you can do to improve the view. If you're looking straight into a fence, hang a garden plaque on the fence, plant something green and lush in front of it, or paint it a beautiful color. If you look out onto a parking lot or busy street, shutter the bottom half of the window, and let the light flood in from above, or hang bird feeders or blooming plants near the window. Highlight views with birdbaths, sculptures, and other "beauty marks," as shown in Figure 17C. Create secret spots that you may only be able to see from one window's vantage point, such as the bird-bath shown in Figure 17D. When views are impossible to enhance, or for privacy after dark, fit all your windows with appropriate coverings.

When windows are smaller than you'd like, place a mirror or art with reflective glass across from the window to increase the natural light. Hang a faceted crystal in or near the window to attract and circulate Ch'i.

Skylights are recommended in active rooms such as living rooms, offices, family rooms, kitchens, garages, and bathrooms—but not direct-ly over your bed, desk, or dining table. Skylights tend to activate the upward flow of Ch'i, making it difficult to sit or rest beneath them for any length of time. If there is a skylight located above a favorite piece of fur-niture, rearrange the room, or install a shade that can be adjusted as nec-essary.

As with mirrors, large single-paned windows present you with a clear, whole view. Stained glass, used as art, not as a viewing window, can be as ornate as you like. All windows should be kept clean and in good repair, including windows in garages, basements, attics, and other out-of-the-way places.


### Doors

Your front door, often referred to as the "Mouth of Ch'i," is considered the primary opening through which vital energy and favorable opportu-nities flow into your life. All other doors are seen as smaller "mouths" where, like fresh air, Ch'i finds its way into the rooms of your home.

When building a home or addition, plan on doing one of two things. Either locate your doors so that they are not directly across from other doors or large windows, or leave enough room to locate a piece of fur-niture, planter, island, sculpture, or screen between them. As with win-dows, when doors are located directly across from other doors, the ener-gy streams too quickly through the room, unless slowed and circulated by something substantial between them. You want Ch'i to meander around a room like a refreshing breeze, rather than blowing straight through like a strong wind.

Give doors that open into a confined space, such as a hall or foyer, a view that opens up the space. This can be done with a mirror or art that has depth, as shown in Figure 16A, page 224. Almost any confined space can be made more inviting and interesting in this way.

The area around any door should be well lit. Make sure lights or light switches are conveniently located near all your doors, including those in halls, basements, and attics. Check all the doors in your home to make sure they open fully and easily. Anything that inhibits a door's full range of motion needs to be relocated. Repair doors as soon as you notice they are sticky, rickety, or in need of new hardware or paint.

### Quick Reference Guidelines for Windows and Doors

- Modulate Ch'i flow between windows and doors.
- Beautify views.
- Treat windows and doors for privacy.
- Choose single-paned (single-light) windows when possible.
- Keep all windows and doors in good repair.
- Locate light switches conveniently near doors.

# Chapter Eighteen

# CLEANSINGS AND BLESSINGS— BATHING THE SOUL OF YOUR HOME

*"May I be peaceful and at ease*
*May my home be filled with loving kindness*
*May it be a safe haven*
*May I be happy*
*At home, in the present moment."*
—Jack Kornfield

### Cleaning and Cleansing First

Cleaning our homes cleanses them of not only dirt and clutter, but also of stagnant, unhealthy energy. There are times, however, when a room looks clean but doesn't feel clean. There's a stale, sticky, or spooky feeling that clings to the room even after a normal cleaning. Many people feel this in older homes where several generations of people have lived. Others notice an unclean feeling when they move into a newer home that was previously occupied. Some people are sensitive enough to feel the energetic leftovers in a room where there's been an argument, or where someone was emotionally troubled or died. In these cases, it's important to energetically cleanse the room as well as physically clean it.

**FIGURE 18A**

*These candles have been grouped together to represent the Five Elements and to cleanse and purify the energy in the room.*
***(Also in color, page 128.)***

When moving into a home that's been previously occupied, always deep-clean the carpets and paint the walls immediately. In most cases, this removes the energy of the people who lived there before you, and puts your personal signature on your "new" home. Then, spray a cleansing mist along the baseboards and into all the corners of your home to refresh and rejuvenate the Ch'i. Cleansing mists contain citrus oil and can be purchased where aromatherapy products are sold, or you can make your own by putting several drops of orange or lemon oil in an atomizer filled with water (other oils can also be added). Or, boil two cups of water, remove from the heat, and add the peel of an orange or a lemon. Let it cool, strain the peels, and put the water into an atomizer.

You can also tap into the power of the Five Elements when doing a cleansing (Chapter 3). For cleansing purposes, you can gather them together to create a "power" grouping in as simple or elaborate an arrangement as you'd like. Figure 18A shows a tray of candles that combines all the elements with the intention to cleanse the room. A red candle (Fire) and yellow flower petals (Earth and Wood) floating in a silver bowl of water (Metal and Water) is one of countless examples of an elemental combination that can be used for cleansing purposes. Consider how *you* would combine the elements to create a cleansing arrangement.

Use this list when choosing elemental components to cleanse a room:

### *Wood:*

- Items made from wood
- Sage (burnt like incense, or placed in hot water to diffuse aromatic oils)
- Natural incenses made from barks and flowers
- Essential oils from flowers and fruits
- Citrus peel
- Fresh flowers, flower petals, plants
- Cloths made from plant fibers, such as cotton, linen, and rayon
- Items that are in blue and green tones, and/or are columnar in shape

### *Fire:*

- Candles
- Electric and oil lamps
- Figurines of people or animals
- Items made from animals, such as leather, bone, and feathers
- Cloths made from animal fibers, such as wool and silk
- Items that are in red tones and/or are triangular in shape

### *Earth:*

- Ceramic and earthenware figures, tiles, and vessels
- Clay or soil, often taken from a special place
- Items that are in yellow or earthtones, and/or are square in shape

### Metal:

- Metal figures and vessels
- Salt and Epsom Salts
- Natural crystals
- Rocks and stones
- Items that are white, very light pastels, and/or are round in shape

### Water:

- Pure, clean water and water features
- Items made from glass or crystal, such as vases, bowls, and candleholders
- Mirrors
- Items that are black, have very dark tones, and/or are free-flowing in shape

Experiment with arranging items in the room you're cleansing until you find a combination that really pleases you. If you have included candles in your grouping, make sure they can safely burn for at least an hour. When you are satisfied with your arrangement, light any candles, and affirm your intention to purify and balance the room, knowing that your arrangement amplifies your wishes. Let it remain for at least one hour or longer when appropriate, then remove and discard "disposables" such as water and petals. Thoroughly wash all vessels, and cleanse items such as figurines and stones by placing them in the sun for a day.

In extremely rare cases, when ghosts or poltergeists are suspected, you'll need the expertise of someone who specializes in exorcisms. Typically, you can rely on the Five Elements and your own focused intention to transform your rooms into places filled with light and good energy.

### House Blessings

Blessings have been a part of all cultures since the beginning of time, infusing many of our life passages with purpose and spiritual substance. It is important to remember that no matter how many times blessings are said or performed, only *you* can give them meaning. It is your vital energy and full participation that activates blessings and good wishes. In essence, *you are the blessing.*

In Feng Shui, when you bless your home, you are blessing the dynamic being who shelters you every day. Your home *deserves* to be honored, blessed, and celebrated. Housewarmings are a popular way to bless a new home, but what comes after that? Make sure you bless your home frequently with your thoughts and actions. Put your home on your gratitude list, and write down all the things you love about it.

Blessing ceremonies abound in every religion and spiritual discipline. Choose one that feels right, or create your own. Give your house a name, celebrate its birthday, and baptize it with water and prayers. Invite your friends to come and help you bless and celebrate your home sweet home. Make sure it's clean prior to performing any official blessing, preparing it much as you would prepare yourself by bathing before a special occasion.

Remember that, essentially, you are the blessing. The quality of your inner life is directly reflected in your home. No amount of external blessings will bring light into your home if you are unwilling to carry it within you.

---

**CONTEMPLATIVE EXERCISE**

CONNECT WITH THE DEEP WELLSPRING OF YOUR SPIRIT, AND CLAIM THE POWER TO BESTOW BLESSINGS UPON YOURSELF AND OTHERS. MEDITATE ON EXACTLY WHAT YOU CAN DO TO BLESS YOUR HOME. IT MAY BE A PRAYERFUL LIGHTING OF CANDLES IN EACH ROOM; A CIRCLE OF FRIENDS GATHERED TO BLESS YOUR HOME WITH YOU; OR A CELEBRATION THAT INCLUDES FOOD, MUSIC, AND DANCE. BLESS YOUR HOME, WHILE BEING FULLY AWARE THAT YOUR WHOLE LIFE IS A BLESSING.

---

# *Chapter 19*

# CH'I REPLENISHING EXERCISES— NOURISHING THE CH'I WITHIN

*"Stay full, stay in the state of love. Remember that once
you achieve this state of love, nothing nor anyone can
pull more energy from you than you can replace."*
— James Redfield

Ch'i—vital energy—animates every person, place, and thing. That's why Feng Shui focuses on enhancing the Ch'i in ourselves and in our homes. We arrange our furniture and possessions to promote good energy flow, live with what we love, and choose designs that are safe and comfortable. We simplify our environments to encourage creative self-expression and clarity of purpose.

Along with your environmental improvements, remember to attend to your inner balance. Here are two simple meditative exercises for gathering and replenishing your Ch'i. The first one can be practiced at any time. For the second exercise, you'll need a special spot.

### Sphere of Ch'i Exercise

This valuable Ch'i replenishment Exercise can be practiced any-where, anytime.

*To begin: Stand, sit, or lie down quietly, and breathe slowly and deeply. Visualize a bright golden sphere of energy, like pure sunshine, encircling your body. This is your Sphere of Ch'i. Relax and visualize this sphere radiating pure life force into every part of your body. Inhale deeply and exhale any feelings of tension. Inhale and visualize your sphere of Ch'i filling and replenishing every part of your body, mind, and spirit with healing, rejuvenating energy. Exhale completely and inhale again, sending vital energy to the parts of the your body—or your life—where it is needed, and filling any painful space with energy and light. Exhale everything you want to let go of. Continue to breathe deeply, and nourish your whole being with the healing energy of your Sphere of Ch'i.*

You can replenish your Ch'i at any time using this simple technique. It is the perfect antidote to stress, and it can rejuvenate you whenever you're feeling depleted.

### Ch'i Movement Exercise

This active exercise works especially well when accompanied by drumming or upbeat music.

*Stand with your feet about shoulder-width apart. Notice how you feel as you stand listening to the music. Then, allow your body to move and shake to the rhythm of the music. Let your arms, your head, your knees, and your whole body be involved in the sensations of moving, shaking, and bouncing. This is not a dance routine that's supposed to look good, but rather spontaneous movement of the body to release ten-sion and gather Ch'i. Shake your feet one at a time. Let your back move and bounce, shaking out tension and stress from every vertebra. Let go, then let go again and again. Now stop and stand still. You'll feel the tingling presence of Ch'i flowing through every part of your body. If you have the time, sit or lie down and do the Sphere of Ch'i exercise.*

This movement exercise can be done for one to fifteen minutes in private or in a movement class. It's also quite fun to do with children.

# *Afterword*

*"We must be willing to get rid of the life we've planned,
so as to have the life that is waiting for us."*
— Joseph Campbell

A year ago, I spent a month in the heart of England's Lake District on a writing holiday. It was the height of spring, and in 30 days it rained only once. There was one view in particular, from the back of Sawrey House, that was truly remarkable. From my vantage point, the land spread out like an emerald blanket in every direction. Newborn oak and maple leaves glistened in the sun, while a riot of colorful azalea and columbine paraded down to a cutting garden wrapped in pink rhodo-dendron. Purple wisteria and white lilacs spilled their sweetness into the breeze, and bees droned from flower to flower. Beyond the garden, pastures led to ancient trees strung along the glittering body of Lake Esthwaite. Across the lake, the gentle hills of Grisedale Forest rose in every shade of green. A cool breeze moved everything in a slow waltz. It was heaven on earth.

I have always believed that life can be heaven on earth, and that through loving thoughts, words, and actions, I could create it. And I believe that this is true for us all if we choose it. Depending on the circumstances, though, the decision to create a heavenly life can begin with some hellish times.

A decade ago I moved from Washington, D.C., to San Diego. As I headed west, I knew absolutely that I would not continue my profession (I was a polarity therapy practitioner and teacher). Instead, I settled into my new home and waited for my next set of life instructions. I was married to a man who was also redefining his career, and our dual uncertainty about work produced tremendous tension in our marriage. It was impossible for him to understand how I could be "pregnant with myself" rather than teaching or starting a new practice. To keep some semblance of peace, I got a job with a local greenhouse and continued to wait.

Then a well-meaning friend insisted on dragging me to a lecture on Feng Shui. It was a subject I had tried to read about several times, but each time I'd been frustrated. My frustration ended that day. Dr. Richard Tan was the speaker, and he had spoken for only a few minutes when I realized that this was it! Dr. Tan's every word resonated completely with what I had always intuitively known. The new work I'd been waiting for was about to begin.

The events that followed shortly thereafter were some of the biggest surprises of my life. It began with a great burst of enthusiasm, as I applied what I was learning in Dr. Tan's classes to strengthen and renew my miserable marriage. I enhanced our Love and Marriage area with vibrant flowers, displayed photos of us in happier times, rearranged furniture, and cleared the leftover clutter from our move. I affirmed that my husband and I both deserved to be happy in every way. I was thrilled that I'd discovered how to make our marriage happy again.

Less than 30 days later, I was living in my own studio apartment. The marriage I thought I'd wanted to save ended abruptly within days of my Feng Shui handiwork. In the depths of despair and turmoil, I asked, "What the hell happened?" I was stunned by the how fast my life had changed—and in exactly the way I didn't want it to. Or did I? If I was committed to creating heaven on earth and to living a life of excellence, perhaps this was the path. I had to trust that it was. I realize now that by enhancing the Ch'i flow in my house, our mediocre existence no longer had a place to live. My intention to be happy, coupled with my Feng Shui enhancements, exposed the truth that we really didn't belong together. It was perfect.

I blessed my little apartment, kept only the things that had very positive associations and memories for me, and enhanced the Bagua areas all the way around. This was going to be my mini-paradise for a while. With no troubled relationship to worry about, I was able to dive completely into my Feng Shui studies with Dr. Tan, Louis Audet, and Master Lin Yun. I also read every book on Feng Shui I could find, assimilating and integrating many of the ideas and techniques into my own practice.

And, I experimented on myself. When I wanted something to happen in my life, I used my clear intention and Feng Shui enhancements to boot-strap my way to a heavenly existence. This included getting a decent job. While affirming that all my needs were abundantly met, I kept the Career area of my apartment clean, clear, and abundantly appointed with flow-ers and flowing water. Soon thereafter, I was offered, and gratefully accepted, a job managing a nearby art gallery.

There, a whole new life unfolded, as opportunities to practice Feng Shui, both in arranging the art gallery and in consulting with customers, flowed my way. I witnessed many people making changes as they embraced Feng Shui, and also watched some of them go through diffi-cult times on their way to creating a better life. My studies and experi-ences excited me enough to start speaking on Feng Shui at local stores, schools, and community centers. It was at one of these lectures that I met Louise Hay. We discovered that we shared an abiding love for many things, including Feng Shui and earthworms, and so a wonderful friend-ship began.

A year passed in a heartbeat, and I was ready for romance. To cele-brate and anchor my intention, I hung a wedding bell wind chime in my Love and Marriage area and decided to rearrange my entire apartment. The day I took everything down from the walls and moved every stick of furniture around, the phone rang. It was Brian Collins, a new acquain-tance, calling to ask me out to lunch. The Chinese saying, "If you want change in your life, move 27 things in your house," took on very real meaning that day. Our lunch marked the beginning of a romance that I'd always believed was possible.

Our relationship had a positive effect on all parts of my life. With every appointment, another Feng Shui story was born, forming the foun-dation of my first book, *The Western Guide to Feng Shui*. Brian, a Feng Shui natural himself, supported me in every way and brought his insights and expert editing skills to my work in progress.

During the Thanksgiving holiday of 1995, Louise Hay presided over our wedding in her candlelit living room. The ceremony fully ground-ed—that is, brought into our everyday lives—heaven on earth. *The Western Guide to Feng Shui* (which I often refer to as our first child) was published by Hay House in the spring of 1996. Soon, requests for Feng Shui education and consultations poured in. To answer the call, I founded

The Western School of Feng Shui, wrote a curriculum, made instructive videos for the Essential Feng Shui practitioners training program, took a million "before and after" slides, designed one-day workshops, and added consultation services and a speakers' bureau. With the Feng Shui momentum in full swing, I wrote *The Western Guide to Feng Shui* Six-Tape Audiocassette Series; the quick reference guide, *Home Design with Feng Shui A–Z;* and, without skipping a beat, this book. I've never worked so hard, been so challenged, or had more fun! Life, complete with its challenges, successes, and quiet times, is heavenly.

Now as I sit in my home office, I look at the life I continue to shape and enjoy. I love the sanctuary of our home and garden, which provides the perfect balance for my hectic work schedule. I am grateful for every opportunity to sow the seeds that encourage and initiate positive change in our world. Certainly, my heaven on earth includes being more involved, stretched, and rewarded than ever before. And the practice of Feng Shui guides my every step.

May it guide yours, too.

# Bibliography/Recommended Reading

*The Celestine Prophecy,* James Redfield. New York: Warner Books, 1994.

*Clear Your Clutter with Feng Shui,* Karen Kingston. New York: Broadway Books, 1998.

*Clutter's Last Stand,* Don Aslett. Cincinnati: Writer's Digest Books, 1984.

*Creating Sacred Space with Feng Shui,* Karen Kingston. New York: Broadway Books, 1997.

*Cultivating Sacred Space,* Elizabeth Murray. Rohnert Park, CA: Pomegranate, 1997.

*The Dynamic Laws of Prosperity,* Catherine Ponder. Englewood Cliffs, NJ: Prentice-Hall, 1973.

*The Essence of Feng Shui,* Jami Lin. Carlsbad, CA: Hay House, 1998.

*The Feng Shui Cookbook,* Elizabeth Miles. Secaucus, NY: Carol Publishing Group, 1998.

*Feng Shui Design,* Sarah Rossbach and Lin Yun. New York: Viking, 1998.

*Feng Shui in Your Garden,* Roni Jay. Boston: Tuttle, 1998.

*Feng Shui Made Easy,* William Spear. New York: Harper-Collins Publishers, 1995.

*Feng Shui Revealed,* R. D. Chin. New York: Clarkson N. Potter, 1998.

*The I Ching or Book of Changes,* Richard Wilhelm & Carey Baynes. Princeton, NJ: Princeton University Press, 1971.

*Healing Environments,* Carol Venolia. Berkeley, CA: Celestial Arts, 1998.

*The Healing House,* Barbara Bannon Harwood. Carlsbad, CA: Hay House, 1997.

*House As a Mirror of Self,* Clare Cooper Marcus. Berkeley, CA: Conari Press, 1995.

*How to Grow Fresh Air,* Dr. B. C. Wolverton. New York: Penguin Books, 1997.

*Interior Design with Feng Shui*, Sarah Rossbach. Toronto: Arkana Books, 1997.

*In the Flow of Life—How to Create and Build Beautiful Water Fountains*, Rick Nichols. Huntington Beach, CA: The Crane's Nest, 1997.

*Kitchens*, Diane Dorrans Saeks. San Francisco: Chronicle Books, 1997.

*Light, Radiation & You*, John N. Ott. Greenwich, CT: Devin-Adder Publishers, 1990.

*Living Color*, Sarah Rossbach & Lin Yun. New York: Kodansha International, 1994.

*Living Rooms*, Diane Dorrans Saeks, San Francisco: Chronicle Books, 1997.

*A Pattern Language*, Christopher Alexander. New York: Oxford University Press, 1977.

*A Room of Her Own*, Chris Casson Madden. New York: Clarkson N. Potter, 1997.

*Sacred Space*, Denise Linn. New York: Ballantine Books, 1995.

*The Sensual Home*, Isle Crawford. New York: Rizzoli International Publications, 1998.

*Shelter for Spirit*, Victoria Moran. New York: Harper-Collins Publishers, 1997.

*Shower of Jewels*, Richard The-Fu Tan, O.M.D.L.Ac and Cheryl Warnke, L.Ac. San Diego: T & W Books, 1996.

*A Soul in Place*, Carol Bridges. Nashville, IN: Earth Nation Publishing, 1995.

*Simple Abundance*, Sarah Ban Breathnach. New York: Warner Books, 1995.

*The Timeless Way of Building*, Christopher Alexander. New York: Oxford University Press, 1979.

*You Can Have It All*, Arnold M. Patent. Hillsboro, OR: Beyond Words Publishing, 1995.

# About the Author

**Terah Kathryn Collins** is an internationally recognized Feng Shui author, consultant, speaker, and teacher. Her first book, *The Western Guide to Feng Shui: Creating Balance, Harmony, and Prosperity in Your Environment,* is one of the best-selling Feng Shui books in the world and has been translated into eight languages. Her second book, *Home Design with Feng Shui, A–Z,* is a colorfully illustrated quick reference guide; while her third, *The Western Guide to Feng Shui, Room by Room,* contains more than 100 photographs on the subject. Terah's *Feng Shui Personal Paradise Cards* feature an informative booklet and 54 colorful flash cards that explain all of the Feng Shui basics.

Terah is the founder of the Western School of Feng Shui in Solana Beach, California, and the originator of Essential Feng Shui®, which focuses on the many practical applications Feng Shui has to offer our Western culture. Featured on the PBS *Body and Soul* series, Terah has spoken at numerous special events, including the New Millennium Conference in Mexico, Magical Mastery and Today's Wisdom Tours in Australia, and the Empowering Women Conferences across the United States.

## More Ways to Enjoy the Benefits of Feng Shui

Whether you want to transform your residence into a personal paradise, your office into a powerhouse of productivity, or you're searching for a rewarding new career, Western School of Feng Shui can light your way. We offer:

- Practitioner Training
- Essential Feng Shui® Workshops
- Professional Consultations for Residences and Business
- Feng Shui Speakers for Group Presentations
- Feng Shui Products at the "Essential Feng Shui Gallery"

### Western School of Feng Shui™
Terah Kathryn Collins, Founder

More Results, Less Mystery
Essential Feng Shui® Practitioner Training Program

Since 1996, Western School of Feng Shui has offered training for men and women who are interested in becoming practitioners or who want to add Feng Shui to their current career. This unique and practical program is founded upon the principles presented in Terah's books. The training is for anyone who feels committed to enrich his or her life, or who wants to embark on a nurturing and rewarding full-time or part-time career path.

"Feng Shui Marketing" is included as a vital component of the training, enabling graduates to turn their knowledge into tangible real-world success. Students and graduates have the opportunity to participate in optional programs designed to support a prosperous Feng Shui practice, including a mentor program, speakers bureau, workshop presentation opportunities, consultation referrals, online directory listing and chat room, alumni networking, newsletters, and advanced training programs.

*"This is the most comprehensive Feng Shui training that I've found.*
*I feel confident, and my clients are seeing the results."*
— Pamela K. Greer, Del Mar, CA

Visit us at **www.wsfs.com**, or call **800-300-6785** for more information.

Or, write to :
Western School of Feng Shui
P.O. Box 946
Solana Beach, CA 92075

*Western School of Feng Shui draws students from across the United States and from more than 26 countries. The commitment they share and the camaraderie they enjoy add a rich dimension to a learning environment filled with intellectual and creative stimulation.*

### *Professional Consultation Services*
### *for Your Residence, Business, or Organization*

Wherever you live or work in the United States or abroad, we can bring the benefits of Feng Shui to your doorstep by referring a seasoned professional Practitioner who is a graduate of Western School of Feng Shui. Our Practitioners are dedicated to getting results while honoring your personal style and taste.

**A consultation for your residence** can create positive changes in health, relationships, and prosperity—and improve the behavior of children.

*"Since Kathryn Voreis came into my life, I have had a much stronger relationship with my husband and we have learned to work together as a team. My career path was finally clarified, resulting in my writing and producing my first book, and now it's distributed by a major bookstore. I definitely believe Feng Shui influenced my life."*
— V.G., Fort Worth, TX

**A consultation for your business** can enhance productivity and profits, reduce stress, improve synergy and creativity, and improve employee retention.

*"When Holly Tashian came into my office and suggested a few simple changes and rearrangements, I was absolutely amazed at the results. What followed was an unbelievable succession of events—large orders, big reviews, checks in the mail, surprising good news via phone calls and, seemingly out of nowhere, we attracted the interest of a large-scale group in New York."*
— M.M, Nashville, TN

**Consultation for organizations and institutions** can increase efficiency, reduce employee turnover and sick leave, help prevent burnout, and improve morale.

*"Since Shivam Kohls came to our nonprofit organization for a Feng Shui consultation, many wonderful things have happened: Within weeks we received over $10K in donations, the county has contacted us about starting our program in other locations, and our morale is up like never before. All this happened with only minor changes and minimal expense. Thank you!"*
— Alan Sorkin, Executive Director, PARTS
(Parents and Adolescents Recovering Together Successfully), San Diego, CA

Find a Feng Shui Practitioner in your area at **www.wsfs.com,** or call **800-300-6785** for a referral (local: **858-793-0945**).

## *Enjoy a Hands-on Feng Shui Learning Experience*

### Feng Shui Essentials™—a Practical Workshop

This unique program is designed for beginning and intermediate students. It offers a powerful, practical approach to a subject often cloaked in mystery. It will deepen your basic knowledge of Feng Shui and give you tools that you can put into immediate use at home and at work. Our program, which includes a slide show with more than 100 images, is presented by skilled Feng Shui teachers and held throughout the U.S. and abroad. It is an excellent fundraising tool and is available to all organizations.

*"Your workshop helped the members of our church understand new ways to bring balance and harmony into our homes and offices—and it helped us raise much-needed funds at a time when our coffers were low. It was a brilliant, inspiring program!"*
— L. Styler, Cleveland, OH

Visit **www.wsfs.com,** or call **800-300-6785** for information.

## *EMPOWER AND INSPIRE YOUR GROUP WITH A LIVE FENG SHUI PRESENTATION*

**Essential Feng Shui® Speakers Bureau**

People in every company and organization are hungry for knowledge that can help them enjoy more healthy, happy, and productive lives. A live Feng Shui presentation arranged through our Speakers Bureau can fill this need by offering remarkable insights and practical tools that are tailored for your group. This is a subject that can captivate any audience, including: corporations, professional and trade organizations, spiritual groups, nonprofit groups, and educational and fraternal organizations. Our skilled presenters can tailor a presentation to fit the needs of your audience.

*"Ellen Schneider of the Western School of Feng Shui Speakers Bureau did a remarkable job of communicating the value of Feng Shui to our business owners. We believe that this information will help our companies grow and prosper and help us all stay balanced in the process. Thanks again."*
— Margy Campbell, National Association of
Women Business Owners, Salt Lake City Chapter

Visit **www.wsfs.com,** or call  **800-300-6785** for information.

## *TREASURES AND TOOLS FOR ENHANCING YOUR LIFE*

**Essential Feng Shui® Gallery**

To cultivate your interest in, or enhance your practice of, Feng Shui, Terah Kathryn Collins has personally selected a rich assortment of high-quality Feng Shui products, now available online through the Essential Feng Shui Gallery. These include:

- Books
- Tapes
- Gifts
- Tools
- Enhancements
- Art

Please visit us at **www.wsfs.com** to view our growing list of offerings.

*Essential Feng Shui® is a registered trademark of Western School of Feng Shui.*

We hope you enjoyed this Hay House book. If you would like to receive a free catalog featuring additional Hay House books and products, or if you would like information about the Hay Foundation, please contact:

**HAY HOUSE**

Hay House, Inc.
P.O. Box 5100
Carlsbad, CA 92018-5100

**(760) 431-7695** or **(800) 654-5126**
**(760) 431-6948 (fax)** or **(800) 650-5115 (fax)**
**www.hayhouse.com®**

✳ ✳ ✳

*Published and distributed in Australia by:*
Hay House Australia Pty. Ltd. • 18/36 Ralph St. • Alexandria NSW 2015
*Phone:* 612-9669-4299 • *Fax:* 612-9669-4144 • www.hayhouse.com.au

*Published and distributed in the United Kingdom by:*
Hay House UK, Ltd., 292B Kensal Rd., London W10 5BE
*Phone:* 44-20-8962-1230 • *Fax:* 44-20-8962-1239 • www.hayhouse.co.uk

*Published and distributed in the Republic of South Africa by:*
Hay House SA (Pty), Ltd., P.O. Box 990, Witkoppen 2068
*Phone/Fax:* 27-11-706-6612 • orders@psdprom.co.za

*Published in India by:*
Hay House Publishers India, Muskaan Complex, Plot No. 3, B-2, Vasant Kunj,
New Delhi 110 070 • *Phone:* 91-11-4176-1620
*Fax:* 91-11-4176-1630 • www.hayhouseindia.co.in

*Distributed in Canada by:*
Raincoast , 9050 Shaughnessy St., Vancouver, B.C. V6P 6E5
*Phone:* (604) 323-7100 • *Fax:* (604) 323-2600 • www.raincoast.com

✳ ✳ ✳

Tune in to **HayHouseRadio.com®** for the best in inspirational talk radio featuring top Hay House authors! And, sign up via the Hay House USA Website to receive the Hay House online newsletter and stay informed about what's going on with your favorite authors. You'll receive bimonthly announcements about: Discounts and Offers, Special Events, Product Highlights, Free Excerpts, Giveaways, and more!
**www.hayhouse.com®**